CREDITS

cK-12

We also thank the amazing Utah science teachers whose collaborative efforts made the book possible. Thank you for your commitment to science education and Utah students!

THIS BOOK IS YOURS TO KEEP, SO WRITE ON ALL THE PAGES YOU LIKE. THERE'S EVEN SPACE ON THE BACK COVER FOR YOUR NAME.

IT'S YOUR LEARNING, IT'S YOUR BOOK. ENJOY.

This is your space for drawing, taking notes and making the book your own as you learn.

TABLE OF CONTENTS

UTAH SCIENCE CORE CURRICULUM ALIGNMENT

STANDARD 1: STUDENTS WILL UNDERSTAND THE SCIENTIFIC EVIDENCE THAT SUPPORTS THEORIES THAT EXPLAIN HOW THE UNIVERSE AND THE SOLAR SYSTEM DEVELOPED. THEY WILL COMPARE EARTH TO OTHER OBJECTS IN THE SOLAR SYSTEM.

Objective 1: Describe both the big bang theory of universe formation and the nebular theory of solar system formation and evidence supporting them. **(P. 13)**

a) Identify the scientific evidence for the age of the solar system (4.6 billion years), including Earth (e.g., radioactive decay).
b) Describe the big bang theory and the evidence that supports this theory (e.g., cosmic background radiation, abundance of elements, distance/redshift relation for galaxies).
c) Describe the nebular theory of solar system formation and the evidence supporting it (e.g., solar system structure due to gravity, motion and temperature; composition and age of meteorites; observations of newly forming stars).
d) Explain that heavy elements found on Earth are formed in stars.

e) Investigate and report how science has changed the accepted ideas regarding the nature of the universe throughout history.
f) Provide an example of how technology has helped scientists investigate the universe.

Objective 2: Analyze Earth as part of the solar system, which is part of the Milky Way galaxy. **(P. 24)**

a) Relate the composition of objects in the solar system to their distance from the Sun.
b) Compare the size of the solar system to the Milky Way galaxy.
c) Compare the size and scale of objects within the solar system.
d) Evaluate the conditions that currently support life on Earth (biosphere) and compare them to the conditions that exist on other planets and moons in the solar system (e.g., atmosphere, hydrosphere, geosphere, amounts of incoming solar energy, habitable zone).

STANDARD 2: STUDENTS WILL UNDERSTAND EARTH'S INTERNAL STRUCTURE AND THE DYNAMIC NATURE OF THE TECTONIC PLATES THAT FORM ITS SURFACE.

Objective 1: Evaluate the source of Earth's internal heat and the evidence of Earth's internal structure. (P. 60)

a) Identify that radioactive decay and heat of formation are the sources of Earth's internal heat.

b) Trace the lines of scientific evidence (e.g., seismic studies, composition of meteorites, and samples of the crust and mantle) that led to the inference that Earth's core, mantle, and crust are separated based on composition.

c) Trace the lines of scientific evidence that led to the inference that Earth's lithosphere, asthenosphere, mesosphere, outer core, and inner core are separated based on physical properties.

d) Model how convection currents help distribute heat within the mantle.

Objective 2: Describe the development of the current theory of plate tectonics and the evidence that supports this theory. (P. 70)

a) Explain Alfred Wegener's continental drift hypothesis, his evidence (e.g., fossil record, ancient climates, geometric fit of continents), and why it was not accepted in his time.

b) Cite examples of how the geologic record preserves evidence of past change.

c) Establish the importance of the discovery of mid-ocean ridges, oceanic trenches, and magnetic striping of the sea floor to the development of the modern theory of plate tectonics.

d) Explain how mantle plumes (hot spots) provide evidence for the rate and direction of tectonic plate motion.

e) Organize and evaluate the evidence for the current theory of plate tectonics: sea floor spreading, age of sea floor, distribution of earthquakes and volcanoes.

Objective 3: Demonstrate how the motion of tectonic plates affects Earth and living things. (P. 94)

a) Describe a lithospheric plate and identify the major plates of the Earth.

b) Describe how earthquakes and volcanoes transfer energy from Earth's interior to the surface (e.g., seismic waves transfer mechanical energy, flowing magma transfers heat and mechanical energy).

c) Model the factors that cause tectonic plates to move (e.g., gravity, density, convection).

d) Model tectonic plate movement and compare the results of plate movement along convergent, divergent, and transform boundaries (e.g., mountain building, volcanoes, earthquakes, mid-ocean ridges, oceanic trenches).

e) Design, build, and test a model that investigates local geologic processes (e.g., mudslides, earthquakes, flooding, erosion) and the possible effects on human- engineered structures (e.g., dams, homes, bridges, roads).

STANDARD 3: STUDENTS WILL UNDERSTAND THE ATMOSPHERIC PROCESSES THAT SUPPORT LIFE AND CAUSE WEATHER AND CLIMATE.

Objective 1: Relate how energy from the Sun drives atmospheric processes and how atmospheric currents transport matter and transfer energy. (P. 104)

a) Compare and contrast the amount of energy coming from the Sun that is reflected, absorbed or scattered by the atmosphere, oceans, and land masses.

b) Construct a model that demonstrates how the greenhouse effect contributes to atmospheric energy.

c) Conduct an investigation on how the tilt of Earth's axis causes variations in the intensity and duration of sunlight striking Earth.

d) Explain how uneven heating of Earth's atmosphere at the equator and polar regions combined with the Coriolis effect create an atmospheric circulation system including, Hadley cells, trade winds, and prevailing westerlies, that moves heat energy around Earth.

e) Explain how the presence of ozone in the stratosphere is beneficial to life, while ozone in the troposphere is considered an air pollutant.

Objective 2: Describe elements of weather and the factors that cause them to vary from day to day. (P. 123)

a) Identify the elements of weather and the instruments used to measure them (e.g., temperature-thermometer; precipitation-rain gauge or Doppler radar; humidity-hygrometer; air pressure-barometer; wind-anemometer; cloud coverage-satellite imaging).

b) Describe conditions that give rise to severe weather phenomena (e.g., thunderstorms, tornados, hurricanes, El Niño/La Niña).

c) Explain a difference between a low pressure system and a high pressure system, including the weather associated with them.

d) Diagram and describe cold, warm, occluded, and stationary boundaries (weather fronts) between air masses.

e) Design and conduct a weather investigation, use an appropriate display of the data, and interpret the observations and data.

Objective 3: Examine the natural and human-caused processes that cause Earth's climate to change over intervals of time ranging from decades to millennia. (P. 145)

a) Explain differences between weather and climate and the methods used to investigate evidence for changes in climate (e.g., ice core sampling, tree rings, historical temperature measurements, changes in the extent of alpine glaciers, changes in the extent of Arctic sea ice).

b) Explain how Earth's climate has changed over time and describe the natural causes for these changes (e.g., Milankovitch cycles, solar fluctuations, plate tectonics).

c) Describe how human activity influences the carbon cycle and may contribute to climate change.

d) Explain the differences between air pollution and climate change and how these are related to society's use of fossil fuels. 7. Investigate the current and potential consequences of climate change (e.g., ocean acidification, sea level rise, desertification, habitat loss) on ecosystems, including human communities.

STANDARD 4: STUDENTS WILL UNDERSTAND THE DYNAMICS OF THE HYDROSPHERE.

Objective 1: Characterize the water cycle in terms of its reservoirs, water movement among reservoirs and how water has been recycled throughout time. (P. 150)

a) Identify oceans, lakes, running water, frozen water, ground water, and atmospheric moisture as the reservoirs of Earth's water cycle, and graph or chart the relative amounts of water in each.
b) Describe how the processes of evaporation, condensation, precipitation, surface runoff, ground infiltration and transpiration contribute to the cycling of water through Earth's reservoirs.
c) Model the natural purification of water as it moves through the water cycle and compare natural purification to processes used in local sewage treatment plants.

Objective 2: Analyze the characteristics and importance of freshwater found on Earth's surface and its effect on living systems. (P. 180)

a) Investigate the properties of water: exists in all three states, dissolves many substances, exhibits adhesion and cohesion, density of solid vs. liquid water.
b) Plan and conduct an experiment to investigate biotic and abiotic factors that affect freshwater ecosystems.

c) Using data collected from local water systems, evaluate water quality and conclude how pollution can make water unavailable or unsuitable for life.
d) Research and report how communities manage water resources (e.g., distribution, shortages, quality, flood control) to address social, economic, and environmental concerns.

Objective 3: Analyze the physical, chemical, and biological dynamics of the oceans and the flow of energy through the oceans. (P. 194)

a) Research how the oceans formed from outgassing by volcanoes and ice from comets.
b) Investigate how salinity, temperature, and pressure at different depths and locations in oceans and lakes affect saltwater ecosystems.
c) Design and conduct an experiment comparing chemical properties(e.g., chemical composition, percent salinity) and physical properties(e.g., density, freezing point depression) of freshwater samples to saltwater samples from different sources.
d) Model energy flow in the physical dynamics of oceans (e.g., wave action, deep ocean tides circulation, surface currents, land and sea breezes, El Niño, upwellings).
e) Evaluate the impact of human activities (e.g., sediment, pollution, overfishing) on ocean systems.

STANDARD 5: STUDENTS WILL UNDERSTAND HOW EARTH SCIENCE INTERACTS WITH SOCIETY.

Objective 1: Characterize Earth as a changing and complex system of interacting spheres. (P. 212)

a) Illustrate how energy flowing and matter cycling within Earth's biosphere, geosphere, atmosphere, and hydrosphere give rise to processes that shape Earth.

b) Explain how Earth's systems are dynamic and continually react to natural and human caused changes.

c) Explain how technological advances lead to increased human knowledge (e.g., satellite imaging, deep sea ocean probes, seismic sensors, weather radar systems) and ability to predict how changes affect Earth's systems.

d) Design and conduct an experiment that investigates how Earth's biosphere, geosphere, atmosphere, or hydrosphere reacts to human-caused change.

e) Research and report on how scientists study feedback loops to inform the public about Earth's interacting systems.

Objective 2: Describe how humans depend on Earth's resources. (P. 217)

a) Investigate how Earth's resources (e.g., mineral resources, petroleum resources, alternative energy resources, water resources, soil and agricultural resources) are distributed across the state, the country, and the world.

b) Research and report on how human populations depend on Earth resources for sustenance and how changing conditions over time have affected these resources (e.g., water pollution, air pollution, increases in population).

c) Predict how resource development and use alters Earth systems (e.g., water reservoirs, alternative energy sources, wildlife preserves).

d) Describe the role of scientists in providing data that informs the discussion of Earth resource use.

e) Justify the claim that Earth science literacy can help the public make informed choices related to the extraction and use of natural resources.

Objective 3: Indicate how natural hazards pose risks to humans. (P. 233)

a) Identify and describe natural hazards that occur locally (e.g., wildfires, landslides, earthquakes, floods, drought) and globally (e.g., volcanoes, tsunamis, hurricanes).

b) Evaluate and give examples of human activities that can contribute to the frequency and intensity of some natural hazards (e.g., construction that may increase erosion, human causes of wildfires, climate change).

c) Document how scientists use technology to continually improve estimates of when and where natural hazards occur.

d) Investigate and report how social, economic, and environmental issues affect decisions about human-engineered structures (e.g., dams, homes, bridges, roads).

UNIVERSE

CHAPTER 1

STANDARD 1: STUDENTS WILL UNDERSTAND THE SCIENTIFIC EVIDENCE THAT SUPPORTS THEORIES THAT EXPLAIN HOW THE UNIVERSE AND THE SOLAR SYSTEM DEVELOPED. THEY WILL COMPARE EARTH TO OTHER OBJECTS IN THE SOLAR SYSTEM.

Standard 1, Objective 1: Describe both the big bang theory of universe formation and the nebular theory of solar system formation and evidence supporting them.

Lesson Objectives
*   Explain the evidence for an expanding universe.
*   Describe the formation of the universe according to the Big Bang Theory.

INTRODUCTION

The study of the universe is called cosmology. Cosmologists study the structure and changes in the present universe. The universe contains all of the star systems, galaxies, gas and dust, plus all the matter and energy that exist. The universe also includes all of space and time.

Evolution of Human Understanding of the Universe

What did the ancient Greeks recognize as the universe? In their model, the universe contained Earth at the center, the Sun, the Moon, five planets, and a sphere to which all the stars were attached. This idea held for many centuries until Galileo's telescope allowed people to recognize that Earth is not the center of the universe. They also found out that there are many more stars than were visible to the naked eye. All of those stars were in the Milky Way Galaxy.

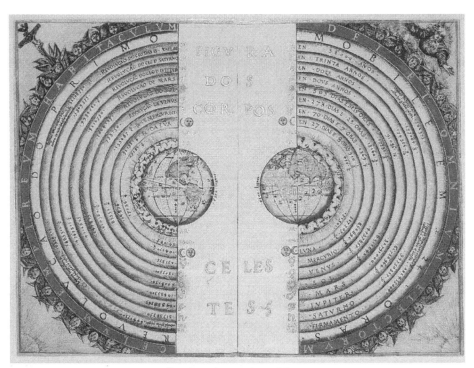

Timeline of cosmological theories

4th century BCE — Aristotle proposes a Geocentric (Earth-centered) universe in which the Earth is stationary and the cosmos (or universe) revolves around the Earth.

2nd century AD — Ptolemy proposes an Earth-centered universe, with the Sun, moon, and visible planets revolving around the Earth.

1543 — Nicolaus Copernicus publishes his heliocentric (Sun-centered) universe theory.

1610 — Johannes Kepler proposes the planets moved around the sun in elliptical orbits.

1687 — Sir Isaac Newton's laws describe large-scale motion throughout the universe

1915 — Albert Einstein publishes the General Theory of Relativity, showing that an energy density warps space and time

1929 — Edwin Hubble demonstrates redshift and thus shows the expansion of the universe

In the early 20th century, an astronomer named Edwin Hubble (1889 – 1953) (see Figure 1 below) discovered that what scientists called the Andromeda Nebula was actually over 2 million light years away — many times farther than the farthest distances that had ever been measured. Hubble realized that many of the objects that astronomers called nebulas were not actually clouds of gas, but were collections of millions or billions of stars — what we now call galaxies.

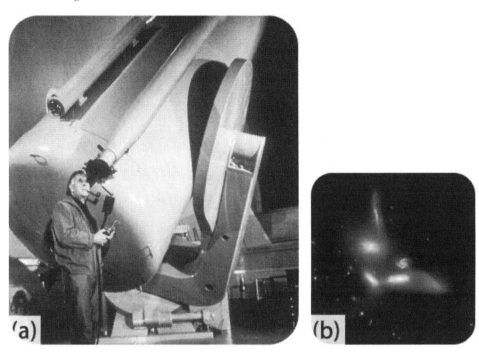

FIGURE 1 (a) Edwin Hubble used the 100-inch reflecting telescope at the Mount Wilson Observatory in California to show that some distant specks of light were galaxies. (b) Hubble's namesake space telescope spotted this six galaxy group. Edwin Hubble demonstrated the existence of galaxies.

Hubble showed that the universe was much larger than our own galaxy. Today, we know that the universe contains about a hundred billion galaxies—about the same number of galaxies as there are stars in the Milky Way Galaxy.

EXPANSION OF THE UNIVERSE

After discovering that there are galaxies beyond the Milky Way, Edwin Hubble went on to measure the distance to hundreds of other galaxies. His data would eventually show how the universe is changing, and would even yield clues as to how the universe formed.

Redshift

If you look at a star through a prism, you will see a spectrum, or a range of colors through the rainbow. The spectrum will have specific dark bands where elements in the star absorb light of certain energies. By examining the arrangement of these dark absorption lines, astronomers can determine the composition of elements that make up a distant star. In fact, the element helium was first discovered in our Sun—not on Earth—by analyzing the absorption lines in the spectrum of the Sun.

While studying the spectrum of light from distant galaxies, astronomers noticed something strange. The dark lines in the spectrum were in the patterns they expected, but they were shifted toward the red end of the spectrum, as shown in the Figure below. This shift of absorption bands toward the red end of the spectrum is known as redshift.

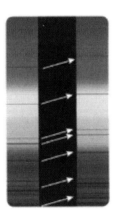

This figure shows the absorption lines in the visible spectrum of a distant galaxy (right), as compared to absorption lines in the visible spectrum of the Sun (left). Arrows indicate redshift. Wavelength increases up towards the red showing the galaxy moving away from the Earth.?

Normal Spectrum of Hydrogen on Earth

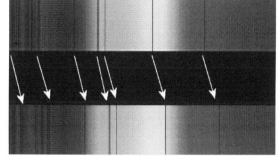

Spectrum of spiral galaxy moving away from Earth

Redshift occurs when the light source is moving away from the observer or when the space between the observer and the source is stretched. What does it mean that stars and galaxies are redshifted? When astronomers see redshift in the light from a galaxy, they know that the galaxy is moving away from Earth.

If galaxies were moving randomly, would some be redshifted and others be blueshifted? Of course. Since almost every galaxy in the universe has a redshift, almost every galaxy is moving away from Earth.

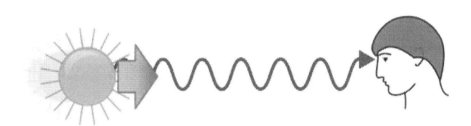

If a source of light is moving away from an observer then the electromagnetic spectrum will be redshifted, If the source is moving toward the observer it is blueshifted.

Redshift can occur with other types of waves too. This phenomenon is called the Doppler Effect. An analogy to redshift is the noise a siren makes as it passes you. You may have noticed that an ambulance seems to lower the pitch of its siren after it passes you. The sound waves shift towards a lower pitch when the ambulance speeds away from you. Though redshift involves light instead of sound, a similar principle operates in both situations.

An animation of Doppler Effect:
http://projects.astro.illinois.edu/data/Doppler/index.html
Youtube video:
http://www.youtube.com/watch?v=Kg9F5pN5tll

THE EXPANDING UNIVERSE

Edwin Hubble combined his measurements of the distances to galaxies with other astronomers' measurements of redshift. From this data, he noticed a relationship, which is now called Hubble's Law: The farther away a galaxy is, the faster it is moving away from us. What could this mean about the universe? It means that the universe is expanding.

The Figure below shows a simplified diagram of the expansion of the universe. One way to picture this is to imagine a balloon covered with tiny dots to represent the galaxies. When you inflate the balloon, the dots slowly move away from each other because the rubber stretches in the space between them. If you were standing on one of the dots, you would see the other dots moving away from you. Also the dots farther away from you on the balloon would move away faster than dots nearby.

Expansion of the Universe Diagram

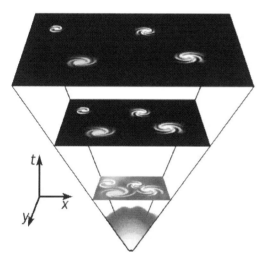

In this diagram of the expansion of the universe over time, the distance between galaxies gets bigger over time, although the size of each galaxy stays the same.

An inflating balloon is only a rough analogy to the expanding universe for several reasons. One important reason is that the surface of a balloon has only two dimensions, while space has three dimensions. But space itself is stretching out between galaxies like the rubber stretches when a balloon is inflated. This stretching of space, which increases the distance between galaxies, is what causes the expansion of the universe.

An animation of an expanding universe is shown here:
http://www.astro.ubc.ca/~scharein/a311/Sim/bang/BigBang.html

One other difference between the universe and a balloon involves the actual size of the galaxies. On the balloon, the dots will become larger in size as you inflate it. In the universe, the galaxies stay the same size, just the space between the galaxies increases.

Formation of the Universe

Before Hubble, most astronomers thought that the universe didn't change. But if the universe is expanding, what does that say about where it was in the past? If the universe is expanding, the next logical thought is that in the past it had to have been smaller.

THE BIG BANG THEORY

The *Big Bang theory* is the most widely accepted cosmological explanation of how the universe formed. If we start at the present and go back into the past, the universe is contracting -- getting smaller and smaller. What is the end result of a contracting universe?

According to the Big Bang theory, the universe began about 13.7 billion years ago. Everything that is now in the universe was squeezed into a very small volume. Imagine the entire known universe compressed into a single, hot, chaotic mass. An explosive expansion — a big bang — caused the universe to start growing rapidly. All the matter and energy in the universe, and even space itself, came out of this expansion.

What came before the Big Bang? There is no way for scientists to know since there is no remaining evidence.

After the Big Bang

In the first few moments after the Big Bang, the universe was unimaginably hot and dense. As the universe expanded, it became less dense and began to cool. After only a few seconds, protons, neutrons, and electrons could form. After a few minutes, those subatomic particles came together to create hydrogen. Energy in the universe was great enough to initiate nuclear fusion and hydrogen nuclei were fused into helium nuclei. The first neutral atoms that included electrons did not form until about 380,000 years later. The matter in the early universe was not smoothly distributed across space. Dense clumps of matter held close together by gravity were spread around. Eventually, these clumps formed countless trillions of stars, billions of galaxies, and other structures that now form most of the visible mass of the universe.

If you look at an image of galaxies at the far edge of what we can see, you are looking at great distances. But you are also looking across a different type of distance. What do those far away galaxies represent? Because it takes so long for light from so far away to reach us, you are also looking back in time. When you look at the stars at night you are actually seeing light from the past as it takes light a very long time (about 186,000 miles per second) to reach us here on Earth.

Approximate light signal travel times

Distance	Time
one foot	1.0 ns
one metre	3.3 ns
from geostationary orbit to Earth	119 ms
the length of Earth's equator	134 ms
from Moon to Earth	1.3 s
from Sun to Earth (1 AU)	8.3 min
from nearest star to Sun (1.3 pc)	4.2 years
from the nearest galaxy (the Canis Major Dwarf Galaxy) to Earth	25,000 years
across the Milky Way	100,000 years
from the Andromeda Galaxy to Earth	2.5 million years

From this table we see that the light we are seeing in our current night sky from the Andromeda Galaxy is actually 2.5 million years old!

After the origin of the Big Bang hypothesis, many astronomers still thought the universe was static (or unmoving). An important line of evidence for the Big Bang was discovered in 1964. In a static universe, the space between objects should have no heat at all; the temperature should measure 0 K (Kelvin is an absolute temperature scale). But two researchers at Bell Laboratories used a microwave receiver to learn that the background radiation in the universe is not 0 K, but 3 K (Figure below). This tiny amount of heat known as cosmic background radiation is left over energy from the Big Bang.

This image shows the cosmic background radiation in the universe as observed from Earth and Space Probes.

How we know about the early universe:
http://www.youtube.com/watch?v=uihNu9lcaeo&feature=channel

History of the Universe, part 2:
http://www.youtube.com/watch?v=bK6_p5a-Hbo&feature=channel

LESSON SUMMARY

- The universe contains all the matter and energy that exists now, that existed in the past, and that will exist in the future. The universe also includes all of space and time.
- Redshift is a shift of element lines toward the red end of the spectrum. Redshift occurs when the source of light is moving away from the observer.
- Light from almost every galaxy is redshifted. The farther away a galaxy is, the more its light is redshifted, and the faster it is moving away from us.
- The redshift of galaxies means that the universe is expanding.
- According to the Big Bang theory, the universe was squeezed into a very small volume and then began expanding explosively about 13.7 billion years ago.
- Cosmic background radiation is left over energy from the Big Bang.

REVIEW QUESTIONS

1. What is redshift, and what causes it to occur? What does redshift indicate?
2. What is the theory of the formation of the universe called?
3. How old is the universe, according to the Big Bang theory?

STANDARD 1, OBJECTIVE 2: ANALYZE EARTH AS PART OF THE SOLAR SYSTEM, WHICH IS PART OF THE MILKY WAY GALAXY.

Lesson Objectives
Classify stars based on their color and temperature.
Outline the stages of a star.

Introduction
When you look at the sky on a clear night, you can see hundreds of stars. A star is a giant ball of glowing gas that is very, very hot. Most of these stars are like our Sun, but some are smaller than our Sun, and some are larger. Except for our own Sun, all stars are so far away that they only look like single points, even through a telescope.

Energy of Stars
Only a tiny bit of the Sun's light reaches Earth, but that light supplies most of the energy at the surface. The Sun is just an ordinary star, but it appears much bigger and brighter than any of the other stars. Of course, this is just because it is very close. Some other stars produce much more energy than the Sun. How do stars generate so much energy?

Nuclear Fusion
Stars shine because of nuclear fusion. Fusion reactions in the Sun's core keep our nearest star burning. Stars are made mostly of hydrogen and helium. Both are very lightweight gases. A star contains so much hydrogen and helium that the weight of these gases is enormous. The pressure at the center of a star is great enough to heat the gases. This causes nuclear fusion reactions.

We call it nuclear fusion because at extreme temperatures of millions of degrees, the collision of atomic nuclei (center) causes the atoms to fuse (join) together. In stars like our Sun, two hydrogen atoms join together to create a helium atom. Nuclear fusion reactions need a lot of energy to get started. Once they begin, they produce even more energy.

Energy from Nuclear Fusion
Nuclear fusion is the opposite of nuclear fission. In fusion, two or more small nuclei combine to form a single, larger nucleus. An example is shown in the Figure right. In this example, two hydrogen nuclei fuse to form a helium nucleus. A neutron and a great deal of energy are also released. In fact, fusion releases even more energy than fission does.

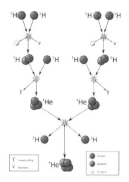

In this nuclear fusion reaction, nuclei of two hydrogen isotopes (tritium and deuterium) fuse together, forming a helium nucleus, a neutron, and energy.

The Power of Stars

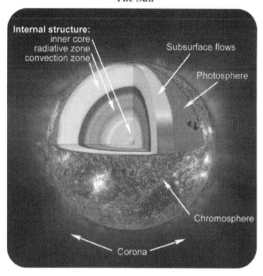

The Sun

Internal structure:
inner core
radiative zone
convection zone
Subsurface flows
Photosphere
Chromosphere
Corona

Nuclear fusion of hydrogen to form helium occurs naturally in the sun and other stars. It takes place only at extremely high temperatures. That's because a great deal of energy is needed to overcome the force of repulsion between positively charged nuclei. The sun's energy comes from fusion in its core, where temperatures reach millions of Kelvin (Figure left).

Hydrogen fuses into helium (in all stars)

Helium fuses into heavier elements (in high-mass stars)

The extremely hot core of the sun radiates energy from nuclear fusion.

HOW STARS ARE CLASSIFIED

Stars shine in many different colors. The color relates to a star's temperature and often its size.

Color and Temperature

Think about the coil of an electric stove as it heats up. The coil changes in color as its temperature rises. When you first turn on the heat, the coil looks black. The air a few inches above the coil begins to feel warm. As the coil gets hotter, it starts to glow a dull red. As it gets even hotter, it becomes a brighter red. Next it turns orange. If it gets extremely hot, it might look yellow-white, or even blue-white. Like a coil on a stove, a star's color is determined by the temperature of the star's surface. Relatively cool stars are red. Warmer stars are orange or yellow. Extremely hot stars are blue or blue-white. (Figure below).

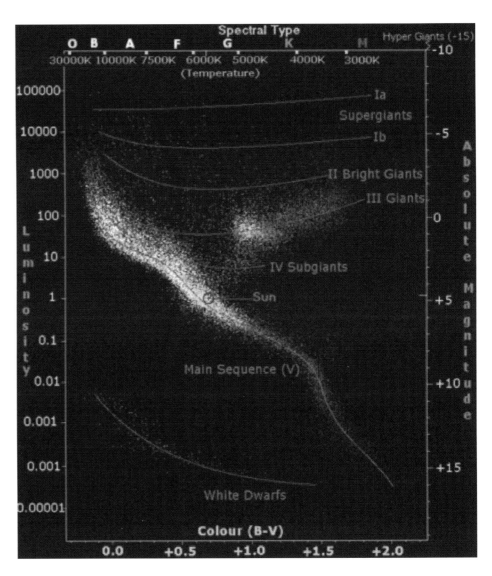

A Hertzsprung-Russell diagram shows the brightness and color of main sequence stars. The brightness is indicated by luminosity and is higher up the y-axis. The temperature is given in degrees Kelvin and is higher on the left side of the x-axis. How does our Sun fare in terms of brightness and color compared with other stars?

Classifying Stars by Color

Color is the most common way to classify stars. The Table below shows the classification system. The class of a star is given by a letter. Each letter corresponds to a color, and also to a range of temperatures. Note that these letters don't match the color names; they are left over from an older system that is no longer used.

For most stars, surface temperature is also related to size. Bigger stars produce more energy, so their surfaces are hotter. Figure on page opposite shows a typical star of each class, with the colors about the same as you would see in the sky.

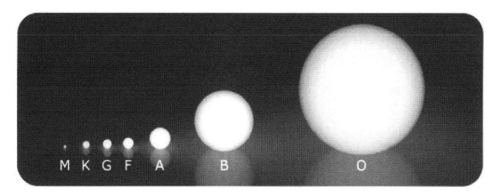

Typical stars by class, color, and size. For most stars, size is related to class and to color. The colors are approximately as they appear in the sky.

LIFETIMES OF STARS

We could say that stars are born, change over time, and eventually die. Most stars change in size, color, and class at least once during their lifetime.

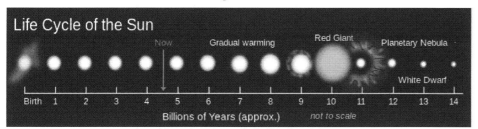

http://en.wikipedia.org/wiki/File:Sun_Life.png

FORMATION OF STARS

Stars are born in clouds of gas and dust called nebulas. Our Sun and solar system formed out of a nebula. A nebula is shown in the Figure left.

Stars form in a nebula like this one in Orion's sword.

27

For a star to form, gravity pulls gas and dust into the center of the nebula. As the material becomes denser, the pressure and the temperature increase. When the temperature of the center becomes hot enough, nuclear fusion begins. The ball of gas has become a star!

Main Sequence Stars

For most of a star's life, hydrogen atoms fuse to form helium atoms. A star like this is a main sequence star. The hotter a main sequence star is, the brighter it is. A star remains on the main sequence as long as it is fusing hydrogen to form helium.

Our Sun has been a main sequence star for about 5 billion years. As a medium-sized star, it will continue to shine for about 5 billion more years. Large stars burn through their supply of hydrogen very quickly. These stars "live fast and die young!" A very large star may only be on the main sequence for 10 million years. A very small star may be on the main sequence for tens to hundreds of billions of years.

Red Giants and White Dwarfs

A star like our Sun will become a red giant in its next stage. When a star uses up its hydrogen, it begins to fuse helium atoms. Helium fuses into heavier atoms like carbon. At this time the star's core starts to collapse inward. The star's outer layers spread out and cool. The result is a larger star that is cooler on the surface, and red in color.

Eventually a red giant burns up all of the helium in its core. What happens next depends on the star's mass. A star like the Sun stops fusion and shrinks into a white dwarf star. A white dwarf is a hot, white, glowing object about the size of Earth. Eventually, a white dwarf cools down and its light fades out. This is the potential end of our star the Sun based on its mass.

Supergiants and Supernovas

A more massive star ends its life in a more dramatic way. Very massive stars become red supergiants, like Betelgeuse.

In a red supergiant, fusion does not stop. Lighter atoms fuse into heavier atoms. Eventually iron atoms form. When there is nothing left to fuse, the star's iron core explodes violently. This is called a supernova explosion. The incredible energy released fuses heavy atoms together. Gold, silver, uranium and the other heavy elements can only form in a supernova explosion. A supernova can shine as brightly as an entire galaxy, but only for a short time, as shown in Figure below. Any element on the periodic table after Iron (atomic number 26) is known as a heavy element.

A supernova, as seen by the Hubble Space Telescope.

Neutron Stars and Black Holes

After a supernova explosion, the star's core is left over. This material is extremely dense. If the core is less than about four times the mass of the Sun, the star will become a neutron star. A neutron star is shown in the Figure below. This type of star is made almost entirely of neutrons. A neutron star has more mass than the Sun, yet it is only a few kilometers in diameter.

A teaspoon of matter from a neutron star would weigh 10 million tons on Earth. If the core remaining after a supernova is more than about 5 times the mass of the Sun, the core collapses to become a black hole. Black holes are so dense that not even light can escape their gravity. For that reason, we can't see black holes. How can we know something exists if radiation can't escape it? We know a black hole is there by the effect that it has on objects around it. Also, some radiation leaks out around its edges. A black hole isn't a hole at all. It is the tremendously dense core of a supermassive star.

LESSON SUMMARY

- A star generates energy by nuclear fusion reactions in its core.
- The color of a star is determined by its surface temperature.
- Stars are classified by color and temperature. The most common system uses the letters O (blue), B (blue-white), A (white), F (yellow-white), G (yellow), K (orange), and M (red), from hottest to coolest.
- Stars form from clouds of gas and dust called nebulas. Nebulas collapse until nuclear fusion starts.
- Stars spend most of their lives on the main sequence, fusing hydrogen into helium.
- Sun-like stars expand into red giants, and then fade out as white dwarf stars.
- Very massive stars expand into red supergiants, explode in supernovas, then end up as neutron stars or black holes.

LESSON REVIEW QUESTIONS

Recall
1. What is nuclear fusion?
2. What do the colors of stars mean?
3. What is a black hole? Why is it called that?

Think Critically
4. Describe the setting in which each of the following elements formed: Hydrogen, Helium, Iron, and Uranium?
5. Describe the Sun's life from its beginning to it eventual end.
6. How do astronomers know how stars form? What evidence do they have?

INTRODUCTION TO THE SOLAR SYSTEM

Lesson Objectives

- Describe some early ideas about our solar system.
- Name the planets, and describe their motion around the Sun.
- Explain how the solar system formed.

Introduction

We can learn a lot about the universe and about Earth history by studying our nearest neighbors. The solar system has planets, asteroids, comets, and even a star for us to see and understand. It's a fascinating place to live!

CHANGING VIEWS OF THE SOLAR SYSTEM

The Sun and all the objects that are held by the Sun's gravity are known as the solar system. These objects all revolve around the Sun. The ancient Greeks recognized five planets. These lights in the night sky changed their position against the background of stars. They appeared to wander. In fact, the word "planet" comes from a Greek word meaning "wanderer." These objects were thought to be important, so they named them after gods from their mythology. The names for the planets Mercury, Venus, Mars, Jupiter, and Saturn came from the names of gods and a goddess.

Earth at the Center of the Universe

The ancient Greeks thought that Earth was at the center of the universe, as shown in the Figure below. The sky had a set of spheres layered on top of one another. Each object in the sky was attached to one of these spheres. The object moved around Earth as that sphere rotated. These spheres contained the Moon, the Sun, and the five planets they recognized: Mercury, Venus, Mars, Jupiter, and Saturn. An outer sphere contained all the stars. The planets appear to move much faster than the stars, so the Greeks placed them closer to Earth. Ptolemy published this model of the solar system around 150 AD.

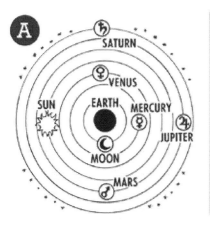

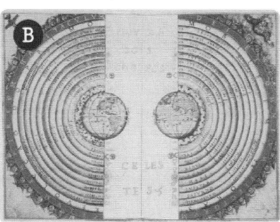

On left is a line art drawing of the Ptolemaic system with Earth at the center. On the right is a drawing of the Ptolemaic system from 1568 by a Portuguese astronomer.

The Sun at the Center of the Universe

About 1,500 years after Ptolemy, Copernicus proposed a startling idea. He suggested that the Sun is at the center of the universe. Copernicus developed his model because it better explained the motions of the planets.

Copernicus proposed a different idea that had the Sun at the center of the universe Copernicus did not publish his new model until his death. He knew that it was heresy to say that Earth was not the center of the universe. It wasn't until Galileo developed his telescope that people would take the Copernican model more seriously. Through his telescope, Galileo saw moons orbiting Jupiter. He proposed that this was like the planets orbiting the Sun.

Planets and Their Motions

Today we know that we have eight planets, five dwarf planets, over 165 moons, and many, many asteroids and other small objects in our solar system. We also know that the Sun is not the center of the universe. But it is the center of the solar system.
The Table below shows our solar system. and gives some data on the mass and diameter of the Sun and planets relative to Earth.

Sizes of Solar System Objects Relative to Earth

Object	Mass (Relative to Earth)	Diameter of Planet (Relative to Earth)
Sun	333,000 Earth's mass	109.2 Earth's diameter
Mercury	0.06 Earth's mass	0.39 Earth's diameter
Venus	0.82 Earth's mass	0.95 Earth's diameter
Earth	1.00 Earth's mass	1.00 Earth's diameter
Mars	0.11 Earth's mass	0.53 Earth's diameter
Jupiter	317.8 Earth's mass	11.21 Earth's diameter
Saturn	95.2 Earth's mass	9.41 Earth's diameter
Uranus	14.6 Earth's mass	3.98 Earth's diameter
Neptune	17.2 Earth's mass	3.81 Earth's diameter

What is (and is not) a planet?

You've probably heard about Pluto. When it was discovered in 1930, Pluto was called the ninth planet. Astronomers later found out that Pluto was not like other planets. For one thing, what they were calling Pluto was not a single object. They were actually seeing Pluto and its moon, Charon. In older telescopes, they looked like one object. This one object looked big enough to be a planet. Alone, Pluto was not very big. Astronomers also discovered many objects like Pluto. They were rocky and icy and there were a whole lot of them.

Astronomers were faced with a problem. They needed to call these other objects planets. Or they needed to decide that Pluto was something else. In 2006, these scientists decided what a planet is. According to the new definition, a *planet* must:

- Orbit a star.
- Be big enough that its own gravity causes it to be round.
- Be small enough that it isn't a star itself.
- Have cleared the area of its orbit of smaller objects.

If the first three are true but not the fourth, then that object is a *dwarf planet*. We now call Pluto a dwarf planet. There are other dwarf planets in the solar system. They are Eris, Ceres, Makemake and Haumea. There are many other reasons why Pluto does not fit with the other planets in our solar system.

The Size and Shape of Orbits

Figure right shows the Sun and planets with the correct sizes. The distances between them are way too small. In general, the farther away from the Sun, the greater the distance from one planet's orbit to the next.

Figure below shows those distances correctly. In the upper left are the orbits of the inner planets and the asteroid belt. The asteroid belt is a collection of many small objects between the orbits of Mars and Jupiter. In the upper right are the orbits of the outer planets and the Kuiper belt. The Kuiper belt is a group of objects beyond the orbit of Neptune.

In this image distances are shown to scale.

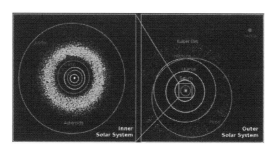

In Figure above, you can see that the orbits of the planets are nearly circular. Pluto's orbit is a much longer ellipse. Some astronomers think Pluto was dragged into its orbit by Neptune.

Distances in the solar system are often measured in astronomical units (AU). One astronomical unit is defined as the distance from Earth to the Sun. 1 AU equals about 150 million km (93 million miles). Table below shows the distance from the Sun to each planet in AU. The table shows how long it takes each planet to spin on its axis. It also shows how long it takes each planet to complete an orbit. Notice how slowly Venus rotates! A day on Venus is actually longer than a year on Venus!

Distances to the Planets and Properties of Orbits Relative to Earth's Orbit

Planet	Average Distance from Sun (AU)	Length of Day (In Earth Days)	Length of Year (In Earth Years)
Mercury	0.39 AU	56.84 days	0.24 years
Venus	0.72	243.02	0.62
Earth	1.00	1.00	1.00
Mars	1.52	1.03	1.88
Jupiter	5.20	0.41	11.86
Saturn	9.54	0.43	29.46
Uranus	19.22	0.72	84.01
Neptune	30.06	0.67	164.8

The Role of Gravity

Planets are held in their orbits by the force of gravity. What would happen without gravity? Imagine that you are swinging a ball on a string in a circular motion. Now let go of the string. The ball will fly away from you in a straight line. It was the string pulling on the ball that kept the ball moving in a circle. The motion of a planet is very similar to the ball on a strong. The force pulling the planet is the pull of gravity between the planet and the Sun.

Every object is attracted to every other object by gravity. The force of gravity between two objects depends on the mass of the objects. It also depends on how far apart the objects are. When you are sitting next to your dog, there is a gravitational force between the two of you. That force is far too weak for you to notice. You can feel the force of gravity between you and Earth because Earth has a lot of mass. The force of gravity between the Sun and planets is also very large. This is because the Sun and the planets are very large objects. Gravity is great enough to hold the planets to the Sun even though the distances between them are enormous. Gravity also holds moons in orbit around planets.

Extrasolar Planets

Since the early 1990s, astronomers have discovered other solar systems. A solar system has one or more planets orbiting one or more stars. We call these planets "extrasolar planets," or "exoplanets". So named because they orbit a star other than the Sun. As of January 2013, 3649 exoplanets have been found. See how many there are now: **http://planetquest.jpl.nasa.gov/**.

We have been able to take pictures of only a few exoplanets. Most are discovered because of some tell-tale signs. One sign is a very slight motion of a star that must be caused by the pull of a planet. Another sign is the partial dimming of a star's light as the planet passes in front of it.

THE NEBULAR THEORY – FORMATION OF THE SOLAR SYSTEM

To figure out how the solar system formed, we need to put together what we have learned. There are two other important features to consider. First, all the planets orbit in nearly the same flat, disk-like region. Second, all the planets orbit in the same direction around the Sun. These two features are clues to how the solar system formed.

A Giant Nebula

Scientists think the solar system formed from a big cloud of gas and dust, called a nebula. This is the solar nebula hypothesis. The nebula was made mostly of hydrogen and helium. There were heavier elements too. Gravity caused the nebula to contract (Figure below). These nebulas may be formed from material leftover from the big bang or recycled from previous supernovas.

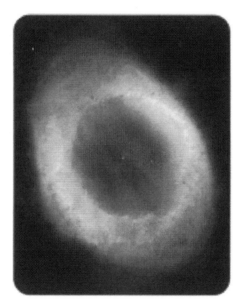

The nebula was drawn together by gravity.

As the nebula contracted, it started to spin. As it got smaller and smaller, it spun faster and faster. This is what happens when an ice skater pulls her arms to her sides during a spin move. She spins faster. The spinning caused the nebula to form into a disk shape. This model explains why all the planets are found in the flat, disk-shaped region. It also explains why all the planets revolve in the same direction. The solar system formed from the nebula about 4.6 billion years ago.

Formation of the Sun and Planets

The Sun was the first object to form in the solar system. Gravity pulled matter together to the center of the disk. Density and pressure increased tremendously. Nuclear fusion reactions begin. In these reactions, the nuclei of atoms come together to form new, heavier chemical elements. Fusion reactions release huge amounts of nuclear energy. From these reactions a star was born, the Sun.

Meanwhile, the outer parts of the disk were cooling off. Small pieces of dust started clumping together. These clumps collided and combined with other clumps. Larger clumps attracted smaller clumps with their gravity. Eventually, all these pieces grew into the planets and moons that we find in our solar system today.

The outer planets — Jupiter, Saturn, Uranus, and Neptune — condensed from lighter materials. Hydrogen, helium, water, ammonia, and methane were among them. It's so cold by Jupiter and beyond that these materials can form solid particles. Closer to the Sun, they are gases. Since the gases can escape, the inner planets — Mercury, Venus, Earth, and Mars — formed from denser elements. These elements are solid even when close to the Sun.

The AGE of the solar system
Based on the age of the oldest meteorites, a group of research scientists at the Institute of Physical Earth Sciences in Paris has carried out very precise measurements of the decay of Uranium 238 to Lead 206. Using radiometric dating we can calculate the age of the Solar System at about 4.56 billion years.

Formation of the Solar System – Stephen Hawking:
http://www.youtube.com/watch?v=Uhy1fucSRQI

The size of the solar system
The universe contains an estimated 100 billion galaxies, of which our Milky Way is one. The Milky Way itself contains an estimated 100 billion stars, of which our Sun is one. The Milky Way is a spiral galaxy with a radius of around 50,000 light-years (a light-year being the distance that light travels in one year), and the Sun and its solar system are around 30,000 light-years from the center of the galaxy.

LESSON SUMMARY

- The Sun and all the objects held by its gravity make up the solar system.
- There are eight planets in the solar system: Mercury, Venus, Earth, Mars, Jupiter, Saturn, and Neptune. Pluto, Eris, Ceres, Makemake and Haumea are dwarf planets.
- The ancient Greeks believed Earth was at the center of the universe and everything else orbited Earth.
- Copernicus proposed that the Sun at the center of the universe and the planets and stars orbit the Sun.
- Planets are held by the force of gravity in elliptical orbits around the Sun.
- The solar system formed from a giant cloud of gas and dust about 4.6 billion years ago.
- This model explains why the planets all lie in one plane and orbit in the same direction around the Sun.

LESSON REVIEW QUESTIONS

Recall
1. What are the names of the 8 planets from the Sun outward?
2. Name 5 of the dwarf planets.
3. How old is the Sun?
4. How old are the Planets?

Apply Concepts
5. Describe the role of gravity in how the solar system functions. Why don't the planets fly off into space? Why don't the planets ram into the sun?
6. Why does the nebular hypothesis explain how the solar system originated?

Think Critically
7. Why do you think so many people for so many centuries thought that Earth was the center of the universe?
8. People were pretty upset when Pluto was made a dwarf planet. Explain why Pluto is now classified as a dwarf planet.

Points to Consider
- Would you expect all the planets in the solar system to be made of similar materials? Why or why not?
- The planets are often divided into two groups: the inner planets and the outer planets. Which planets do you think are in each of these two groups? What do members of each group have in common?

INNER PLANETS

Lesson Objectives

- Describe the main features of each of the inner planets.
- Compare each of the inner planets to Earth and to one another.

Introduction

The four planets closest to the Sun - Mercury, Venus, Earth, and Mars - are referred to as the inner planets. They are similar to Earth. All are solid, dense, and rocky. None of the inner planets have rings. Compared to the outer planets, the inner planets are small. They have shorter orbits around the Sun and they spin more slowly. Venus spins backwards and spins the slowest of all the planets.

All of the inner planets were geologically active at one time. They are all made of cooled igneous rock with inner iron cores. Earth has one big, round moon, while Mars has two very small, irregular moons. Mercury and Venus do not have moons.

MERCURY

Mercury is the smallest planet. It has no moon. The planet is also closest to the Sun. As the Figure below shows, the surface of Mercury is covered with craters, like Earth's moon. The presence of impact craters that are so old means that Mercury hasn't changed much geologically for billions of years. With only a trace of an atmosphere, it has no weather to wear down the ancient craters.

Short year, long days

Mercury is named for the Roman messenger god. Mercury was a messenger because he could run extremely fast. The Greeks gave the planet this name because Mercury moves very quickly in its orbit around the Sun. Mercury orbits the Sun in just 88 Earth days. Mercury has a very short year, but it also has very long days. Mercury rotates slowly on its axis, turning exactly three times for every two times it orbits the Sun. Therefore, each day on Mercury is 58 Earth days long.

Extreme Temperatures

Mercury is very close to the Sun, so it can get very hot. Mercury also has virtually no atmosphere. As the planet rotates very slowly, the temperature varies tremendously. In direct sunlight, the surface can be as hot as 427oC (801oF). On the dark side, the surface can be as cold as –183oC (–297oF)! The coldest temperatures may be on the insides of craters. Most of Mercury is extremely dry. Scientists think that there may be a small amount of water, in the form of ice, at the planet's poles. The poles never receive direct sunlight.

VENUS

Named after the Roman goddess of love, Venus is the only planet named after a female. Venus is sometimes called Earth's "sister planet." But just how similar is Venus to Earth? Venus is our nearest neighbor. Venus is most like Earth in size.

A Harsh Environment

Viewed through a telescope, Venus looks smooth and featureless. The planet is covered by a thick layer of clouds. You can see the clouds in pictures of Venus, such as the Figure below. We make maps of the surface using radar, because the thick clouds won't allow us to take photographs of the surface of Venus.

 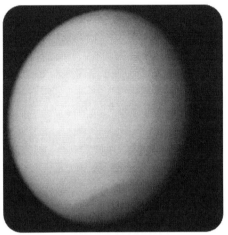

Left - A topographical map of Venus produced by the Magellan probe using radar. Color differences enhance small scale structure.
Right - Venus in real color. The planet is covered by a thick layer of clouds.

The Figure above shows a topographical map of Venus. The map was produced by the Magellan probe on a flyby. Radar waves sent by the spacecraft reveal mountains, valleys, vast lava plains, and canyons. Like Mercury, Venus does not have a moon.

Clouds on Earth are made of water vapor. Venus's clouds are a lot less pleasant. They are made of carbon dioxide, sulfur dioxide and large amounts of corrosive sulfuric acid! The atmosphere of Venus is so thick that the pressure on the surface of Venus is very high. In fact, it is 90 times greater than the pressure at Earth's surface! The thick atmosphere causes a strong greenhouse effect. As a result, Venus is the hottest planet. Even though it is farther from the sun, Venus is much hotter even than Mercury. Temperatures at the surface reach 465oC (860oF). That's hot enough to melt lead!

Volcanoes

Venus has more volcanoes than any other planet. There are between 100,000 and one million volcanoes on Venus! Most of the volcanoes are now inactive. There are also a large number of craters. This means that Venus doesn't have tectonic plates. Plate tectonics on Earth erases features over time.

Motion and Appearance

Venus is the only planet that rotates clockwise as viewed from its North Pole. All of the other planets rotate counterclockwise. Venus turns slowly, making only one turn every 243 days. This is longer than a year on Venus! It takes Venus only 225 days to orbit the Sun.

Because the orbit of Venus is inside Earth's orbit, Venus always appears close to the Sun. You can see Venus rising early in the morning, just before the Sun rises. For this reason, Venus is sometimes called "the morning star." When it sets in the evening, just after the Sun sets, it may be called "the evening star." Since planets only reflect the Sun's light, Venus should not be called a star at all! Venus is very bright because its clouds reflect sunlight very well. Venus is the brightest object in the sky besides the Sun and the Moon.

EARTH

Earth is the third planet out from the Sun, shown in the Figure below. Because it is our planet, we know a lot more about Earth than we do about any other planet. What are main features of Earth?

Oceans and Atmosphere

Earth is a very diverse planet, seen in the Figure above. Water appears as vast oceans of liquid. Water is also seen as ice at the poles or as clouds of vapor. Earth also has large masses of land. Earth's average surface temperature is 14oC (57oF). At this temperature, water is a liquid. The oceans and the atmosphere help keep Earth's surface temperatures fairly steady.

Earth is the only planet known to have life. Conditions on Earth are ideal for life! The atmosphere filters out harmful radiation. Water is abundant. Carbon dioxide was available for early life forms. The evolution of plants introduced more oxygen for animals.

Plate Tectonics

The Earth is divided into many plates. These plates move around on the surface. The plates collide or slide past each other. One may even plunge beneath another. Plate motions cause most geological activity. This activity includes earthquakes, volcanoes, and the buildup of mountains. The reason for plate movement is convection in the mantle. Earth is the only planet that we know has plate tectonics.

Earth's Motions and Moon

Earth rotates on its axis once every 24 hours. This is the length of an Earth day. Earth orbits the Sun once every 365.24 days. This is the length of an Earth year. Earth has one large moon. This satellite orbits Earth once every 29.5 days. This moon is covered with craters, and also has large plains of lava. The Moon came into being from material that flew into space after Earth and a giant asteroid collided. This moon is not a captured asteroid like other moons in the solar system.

Extension: Life on Earth and elsewhere:
nai.arc.nasa.gov/library/downloads/ERG.pdf

MARS

Mars, shown in the Figure below, is the fourth planet from the Sun. The Red Planet is the first planet beyond Earth's orbit. Mars' atmosphere is thin compared to Earth's. This means that there is much lower pressure at the surface. Mars also has a weak greenhouse effect, so temperatures are only slightly higher than they would be if the planet did not have an atmosphere.

Mars is the easiest planet to observe. As a result, it has been studied more than any other planet besides Earth. People can stand on Earth and observe the planet through a telescope. We have also sent many space probes to Mars. In April 2011, there were three scientific satellites in orbit around Mars. The rover, Opportunity, was still moving around on the surface. No humans have ever set foot on Mars. NASA and the European Space Agency have plans to send people to Mars. The goal is to do it sometime between 2030 and 2040. The expense and danger of these missions are phenomenal.

A Red Planet

Viewed from Earth, Mars is red. This is due to large amounts of iron in the soil. The ancient Greeks and Romans named the planet Mars after the god of war. The planet's red color reminded them of blood. Mars has only a very thin atmosphere, made up mostly of carbon dioxide.

Surface Features

Mars is home to the largest volcano in the solar system. Olympus Mons is shown in the Figure below. Olympus Mons is a shield volcano. The volcano is similar to the volcanoes of the Hawaiian Islands. But Olympus Mons is a giant, about 27 km (16.7 miles/88,580 ft) tall. That's three times taller than Mount Everest! At its base, Olympus Mons is about the size of the entire state of Arizona.

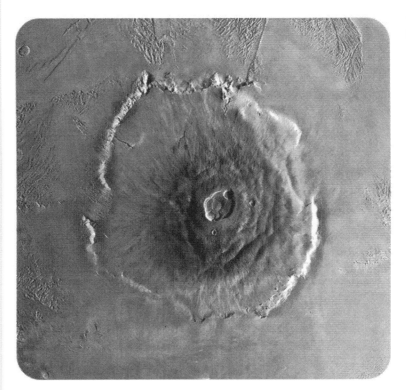

The largest volcano in the solar system, Olympus Mons.

The largest canyon in the solar system, Valles Marineris

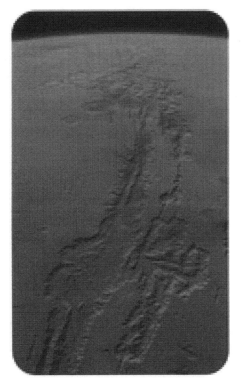

Mars also has the largest canyon in the solar system, Valles Marineris (the Figure below). This canyon is 4,000 km (2,500 miles) long. That's as long as Europe is wide! One-fifth of the circumference of Mars is covered by the canyon. Valles Marineris is 7 km (4.3 miles) deep. How about Earth's Grand Canyon? Earth's most famous canyon is only 446 km (277 miles) long and about 2 km (1.2 miles) deep.

Mars has mountains, canyons, and other features similar to Earth. But it doesn't have as much geological activity as Earth. There is no evidence of plate tectonics on Mars. There are also more craters on Mars than on Earth. But there are fewer craters than on the Moon. What does this suggest to you regarding Mars' plate tectonic history?

Is There Water on Mars?

Water on Mars can't be a liquid. This is because the pressure of the atmosphere is too low. The planet does have a lot of water; it is in the form of ice. The south pole of Mars has a very visible ice cap. Scientists also have evidence that there is also a lot of ice just under the Martian surface. The ice melts when volcanoes erupt. At this times liquid water flows across the surface.

Scientists think that there was once liquid water on the planet. There are many surface features that look like water-eroded canyons. The Mars rover collected round clumps of crystals that, on Earth, usually form in water. If there was liquid water on Mars, life might have existed there in the past.

TWO MARTIAN MOONS

Mars has two very small, irregular moons, Phobos and Deimos. These moons were discovered in 1877. They are named after the two sons of Ares, who followed their father into war. The moons were probably asteroids that were captured by Martian gravity.

LESSON SUMMARY

- The four inner planets are small, dense, solid, rocky planets.
- Mercury is the smallest planet and the closest to the Sun. It has an extremely thin atmosphere so surface temperatures range from very hot to very cold. Like the Moon, it is covered with craters.
- Venus is the second planet from the Sun and the closest planet to Earth, in distance and in size. Venus has a very thick, corrosive atmosphere, and the surface temperature is extremely high.
- Radar maps of Venus show that it has mountains, canyons and volcanoes surrounded by plains of lava.
- Venus rotates slowly in a direction opposite to the direction of its orbit.
- Earth is the third planet from the Sun. It is the only planet with large amounts of liquid water, and the only planet known to support life. Earth is the only inner planet that has a large round moon.
- Mars is the fourth planet from the Sun. It has two small, irregular moons. Mars is red because of rust in its soil. Mars has the largest mountain and the largest canyon in the solar system.
- There is a lot of water ice in the polar ice caps and under the surface of Mars.

LESSON REVIEW QUESTIONS

Recall

1. Name the four inner planets from nearest to the Sun to farthest out from the Sun.
2. Which planet is most like Earth? Why?
3. How do scientists get maps of Venus' surface? What do you see if you look at Venus from Earth through a telescope?

Apply Concepts

4. Which planet do you think has the smallest temperature range? Why?
5. If you were told to go to one of the three inner planets besides Earth to look for life where would you go? Why?

Think Critically

6. Venus is said to have runaway greenhouse effect? Why does it have such a large amount of greenhouse effect? Why do you think is meant by runaway greenhouse effect?

OUTER PLANETS

Lesson Objectives
- Describe main features of the outer planets and their moons.
- Compare the outer planets to each other and to Earth.

Introduction

Jupiter, Saturn, Uranus, and Neptune are the outer planets of our solar system. These are the four planets farthest from the Sun. The outer planets are much larger than the inner planets. Since they are mostly made of gases, they are also called gas giants.

The gas giants are mostly made of hydrogen and helium. These are the same elements that make up most of the Sun. Astronomers think that most of the nebula was hydrogen and helium. The inner planets lost these very light gases. Their gravity was too low to keep them and they floated away into space. The Sun and the outer planets had enough gravity to keep the hydrogen and helium.

All of the outer planets have numerous moons. They also have planetary rings made of dust and other small particles. Only the rings of Saturn can be easily seen from Earth.

JUPITER

Jupiter is the largest planet in our solar system.

Jupiter, shown in the Figure below, is the largest planet in our solar system. Jupiter is named for the king of the gods in Roman mythology.

Jupiter is truly a giant! The planet has 318 times the mass of Earth, and over 1,300 times Earth's volume. So Jupiter is much less dense than Earth. Because Jupiter is so large, it reflects a lot of sunlight. When it is visible, it is the brightest object in the night sky besides the Moon and Venus. Jupiter is quite far from the Earth. The planet is more than five times as far from Earth as the Sun. It takes Jupiter about 12 Earth years to orbit once around the Sun.

A Ball of Gas and Liquid

Since Jupiter is a gas giant, could a spacecraft land on its surface? The answer is no. There is no solid surface at all! Jupiter is made mostly of hydrogen, with some helium, and small amounts of other elements. The outer layers of the planet are gas. Deeper within the planet, the intense pressure condenses the gases into a liquid. Jupiter may have a small rocky core at its center.

A Stormy Atmosphere

Jupiter's atmosphere is unlike any other in the solar system! The upper layer contains clouds of ammonia. The ammonia is different colored bands. These bands rotate around the planet. The ammonia also swirls around in tremendous storms. The Great Red Spot, shown in the Figure above, is Jupiter's most noticeable feature. The spot is an enormous, oval-shaped storm. It is more than three times as wide as the entire Earth! Clouds in the storm rotate counterclockwise. They make one complete turn every six days or so. The Great Red Spot has been on Jupiter for at least 300 years. It may have been observed as early as 1664. It is possible that this storm is a permanent feature on Jupiter. No one knows for sure.

Jupiter's Moons and Rings

Jupiter has lots of moons. As of 2012, we have discovered over 67 natural satellites of Jupiter. Four are big enough and bright enough to be seen from Earth using a pair of binoculars. These four moons were first discovered by Galileo in 1610. They are called the Galilean moons. The Figure below shows the four Galilean moons and their sizes relative to Jupiter's Great Red Spot. These moons are named Io, Europa, Ganymede, and Callisto. The Galilean moons are larger than even the biggest dwarf planets, Pluto and Eris. Ganymede is the biggest moon in the solar system. It is even larger than the planet Mercury!

The Galilean moons are as large as small planets.

Scientists think that Europa is a good place to look for extraterrestrial life. Europa is the smallest of the Galilean moons. The moon's surface is a smooth layer of ice. Scientists think that the ice may sit on top of an ocean of liquid water. How could Europa have liquid water when it is so far from the Sun? Europa is heated by Jupiter. Jupiter's tidal forces are so great that they stretch and squash its moon. This could produce enough heat for there to be liquid water. Numerous missions have been planned to explore Europa, including plans to drill through the ice and send a probe into the ocean. However, no such mission has yet been attempted.

In 1979, two spacecrafts, Voyager 1 and Voyager 2, visited Jupiter and its moons. Photos from the Voyager missions showed that Jupiter has a ring system. This ring system is very faint, so it is very difficult to observe from Earth.

SATURN

Saturn, shown in the Figure right, is famous for its beautiful rings. Saturn is the second largest planet in the solar system. Saturn's mass is about 95 times Earth's mass. The gas giant is 755 times Earth's volume. Despite its large size, Saturn is the least dense planet in our solar system. Saturn is actually less dense than water. This means that if there were a bathtub big enough, Saturn would float! In Roman mythology, Saturn was the father of Jupiter. Saturn orbits the Sun once about every 30 Earth years.

Saturn is the least dense planet in our solar system.
Saturn's composition is similar to Jupiter's. The planet is made mostly of hydrogen and helium. These elements are gases in the outer layers and liquids in the deeper layers. Saturn may also have a small solid core. Saturn's upper atmosphere has clouds in bands of different colors. These clouds rotate rapidly around the planet. But Saturn has fewer storms than Jupiter.

Saturn's Rings

Saturn's rings were first observed by Galileo in 1610. He didn't know they were rings and thought that they were two large moons. One moon was on either side of the planet. In 1659, the Dutch astronomer Christiaan Huygens realized that they were rings circling Saturn's equator. The rings appear tilted. This is because Saturn is tilted about 27 degrees to its side.

The Voyager 1 spacecraft visited Saturn in 1980. Voyager 2 followed in 1981. These probes sent back detailed pictures of Saturn, its rings, and some of its moons. From the Voyager data, we learned that Saturn's rings are made of particles of water and ice with a little bit of dust. There are several gaps in the rings. These gaps were cleared out by moons within the rings. Ring dust and gas are attracted to the moon by its gravity. This leaves a gap in the rings. Other gaps in the rings are caused by the competing forces of Saturn and its moons outside the rings.

Saturn's Moons

As of 2012, over 62 moons have been identified around Saturn. Only seven of Saturn's moons are round. All but one is smaller than Earth's moon. Some of the very small moons are found within the rings. All the particles in the rings are like little moons, because they orbit around Saturn. Someone must decide which ones are large enough to call moons.

Saturn's largest moon, Titan, is about one and a half times the size of Earth's moon. Titan is even larger than the planet Mercury. Scientists are very interested in Titan. The moon has an atmosphere that is thought to be like Earth's first atmosphere. This atmosphere was around before life developed on Earth. Like Jupiter's moon, Europa, Titan may have a layer of liquid water under a layer of ice. Scientists now think that there are lakes on Titan's surface. Don't take a dip, though. These lakes contain liquid methane and ethane instead of water! Methane and ethane are compounds found in natural gas.

Uranus is the 7th planet out from the Sun. Uranus' rings are almost perpendicular to the planet.

URANUS

Uranus, shown in the Figure above, is named for the Greek god of the sky, the father of Saturn. Astronomers pronounce the name "YOOR-uh-nuhs." Uranus was not known to ancient observers. The planet was first discovered with a telescope by the astronomer William Herschel in 1781.

Uranus is faint because it is very far away. Its distance from the Sun is 2.8 billion kilometers (1.8 billion miles). A photon from the Sun takes about 2 hours and 40 minutes to reach Uranus. Uranus orbits the Sun once about every 84 Earth years.

An Icy Blue-Green Ball

Uranus is a lot like Jupiter and Saturn. The planet is composed mainly of hydrogen and helium. There is a thick layer of gas on the outside. Further on the inside is liquid. But Uranus has a higher percentage of icy materials than Jupiter and Saturn. These materials include water, ammonia, and methane. Uranus is also different because of its blue-green color. Clouds of methane filter out red light. This leaves a blue-green color. The atmosphere of Uranus has bands of clouds. These clouds are hard to see in normal light. The result is that the planet looks like a plain blue ball.

Uranus is the least massive outer planet. Its mass is only about 14 times the mass of Earth. Like all of the outer planets, Uranus is much less dense than Earth. Gravity is actually weaker than on Earth's surface. If you were at the top of the clouds on Uranus, you would weigh about 10 percent less than what you weigh on Earth.

The Sideways Planet

All of the planets rotate on their axes in the same direction that they move around the Sun. Except for Uranus. Uranus is tilted on its side. Its axis is almost parallel to its orbit. So Uranus rolls along like a bowling ball as it revolves around the Sun. How did Uranus get this way? Scientists think that the planet was struck and knocked over by another planet-sized object. This collision probably took place billions of years ago.

Rings and Moons of Uranus

Uranus has a faint system of rings, as shown in the Figure below. The rings circle the planet's equator. However, Uranus is tilted on its side. So the rings are almost perpendicular to the planet's orbit.

We have discovered 27 moons around Uranus. All but a few are named for characters from the plays of William Shakespeare.

NEPTUNE

Neptune is shown in the Figure below. It is the eighth planet from the Sun. Neptune is so far away you need a telescope to see it from Earth. Neptune is the most distant planet in our solar system. It is nearly 4.5 billion kilometers (2.8 billion miles) from the Sun. One orbit around the Sun takes Neptune 165 Earth years.

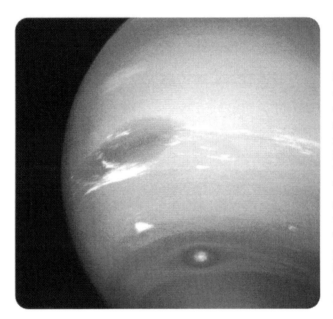

Neptune has a great dark spot at the center left and a small dark spot at the bottom center.

Scientists guessed Neptune's existence before it was discovered. Uranus did not always appear exactly where it should. They said this was because a planet beyond Uranus was pulling on it. This gravitational pull was affecting its orbit. Neptune was discovered in 1846. It was just where scientists predicted it would be! Due to its blue color, the planet was named Neptune for the Roman god of the sea.

Uranus and Neptune are often considered "sister planets." They are very similar to each other. Neptune has slightly more mass than Uranus, but it is slightly smaller in size.

Extremes of Cold and Wind

Like Uranus, Neptune is blue. The blue color is caused by gases in its atmosphere, including methane. Neptune is not a smooth looking ball like Uranus. The planet has a few darker and lighter spots. When Voyager 2 visited Neptune in 1986, there was a large dark-blue spot south of the equator. This spot was called the Great Dark Spot. When the Hubble Space Telescope photographed Neptune in 1994, the Great Dark Spot had disappeared. Another dark spot had appeared north of the equator. Astronomers believe that both of these spots represent gaps in the methane clouds on Neptune.

Neptune's appearance changes due to its turbulent atmosphere. Winds are stronger than on any other planet in the solar system. Wind speeds can reach 1,100 km/h (700 mph). This is close to the speed of sound! The rapid winds surprised astronomers. This is because Neptune receives little energy from the Sun to power weather systems. It is not surprising that Neptune is one of the coldest places in the solar system. Temperatures at the top of the clouds are about −218oC (−360oF).

Neptune's Rings and Moons

Like the other outer planets, Neptune has rings of ice and dust. These rings are much thinner and fainter than Saturn's. Neptune's rings may be unstable. They may change or disappear in a relatively short time.

Neptune has 13 known moons. Only Triton, shown in the Figure below, has enough mass to be round. Triton orbits in the direction opposite to Neptune's orbit. Scientists think Triton did not form around Neptune. The satellite was captured by Neptune's gravity as it passed by.

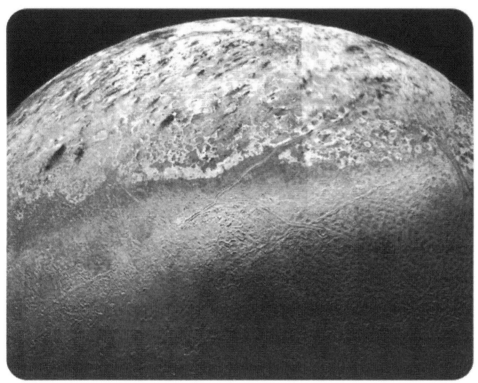

Neptune's moon Triton.

PLUTO

Pluto was once considered one of the outer planets, but when the definition of a planet was changed in 2006, Pluto became one of the dwarf planets. It is one of the largest and brightest objects that make up this group. Look for Pluto in the next lesson, in the discussion of dwarf planets.

LESSON SUMMARY

- The four outer planets — Jupiter, Saturn, Uranus, and Neptune — are all gas giants made mostly of hydrogen and helium. Their thick outer layers are gases and have liquid interiors.
- All of the outer planets have lots of moons, as well as planetary rings made of dust and other particles.
- Jupiter is the largest planet in the solar system. It has bands of different colored clouds, and a long-lasting storm called the Great Red Spot.
- Jupiter has over 60 moons. The four biggest were discovered by Galileo, and are called the Galilean moons.
- One of the Galilean moons, Europa, may have an ocean of liquid water under a layer of ice. The conditions in this ocean might be right for life to have developed.
- Saturn is smaller than Jupiter, but very similar to Jupiter. Saturn has a large system of beautiful rings.
- Saturn's largest moon, Titan, has an atmosphere similar to Earth's atmosphere before life formed.
- Uranus and Neptune were discovered using a telescope. They are similar to each other in size and composition. They are both smaller than Jupiter and Saturn, and also have more icy materials.
- Uranus is tilted on its side, probably due to a collision with a large object in the distant past.
- Neptune is very cold and has very strong winds. It had a large dark spot that disappeared. Another dark spot appeared on another part of the planet. These dark spots are storms in Neptune's atmosphere.

LESSON REVIEW QUESTIONS

RECALL

1. Why were the Galilean moons given that name? What are they?
2.

THINK CRITICALLY

3. How are the outer planets different from the inner planets?
4. If you were given the task of finding life in the outer solar system where would you look?
5. The atmosphere of Saturn's moon Titan because it resembles the early Earth's atmosphere. Why is this interesting to scientists?
6.

POINTS TO CONSIDER

- The inner planets are small and rocky, while the outer planets are large and made of gases. Why might the planets have formed into these two groups?
- We have discussed the Sun, the planets, and the moons of the planets. What other objects can you think of that can be found in our solar system?

OTHER OBJECTS IN THE SOLAR SYSTEM

Lesson Objectives
- **Locate and describe the asteroid belt.**
- **Explain where comets come from and what causes their tails.**
- **Discuss the differences between meteors, meteoroids, and meteorites.**

Introduction

Debris. Space junk. After the Sun and planets formed, there was some material left over. These small chunks didn't get close enough to a large body to be pulled in by its gravity. They now inhabit the solar system as asteroids and comets.

ASTEROIDS

Asteroids are very small, irregularly shaped, rocky bodies. Asteroids orbit the Sun, but they are more like giant rocks than planets. Since they are small, they do not have enough gravity to become round. They are too small to have an atmosphere. With no internal heat, they are not geologically active. An asteroid can only change due to a collision. A collision may cause the asteroid to break up. It may create craters on the asteroid's surface. An asteroid may strike a planet if it comes near enough to be pulled in by its gravity. The Figure below shows a typical asteroid.

Asteroid Ida with its tiny moon Dactyl.

The Asteroid Belt

Hundreds of thousands of asteroids have been found in our solar system. They are still being discovered at a rate of about 5,000 new asteroids per month! The majority are located in between the orbits of Mars and Jupiter. This region is called the asteroid belt, as shown in the Figure below. There are many thousands of asteroids in the asteroid belt. Still, their total mass adds up to only about 4 percent of Earth's moon.

Asteroids formed at the same time as the rest of the solar system. Although there are many in the asteroid belt, they were never were able to form into a planet. Jupiter's gravity kept them apart.

The asteroid belt is between Mars and Jupiter.

Near-Earth Asteroids

Near-Earth asteroids have orbits that cross Earth's orbit. This means that they can collide with Earth. There are over 4,500 known near-Earth asteroids. Small asteroids do sometimes collide with Earth. An asteroid about 5–10 m in diameter hits about once per year. Five hundred to a thousand of the known near-Earth asteroids are much bigger. They are over 1 kilometer in diameter. When large asteroids hit Earth in the past, many organisms died. At times, many species became extinct. Astronomers keep looking for near-Earth asteroids. They hope to predict a possible collision early so they can to try to stop it.

METEORS

If you look at the sky on a dark night, you may see a meteor, like in the Figure below. A meteor forms a streak of light across the sky. People call them shooting stars because that's what they look like. But meteors are not stars at all. The light you see comes from a small piece of matter burning up as it flies through Earth's atmosphere.

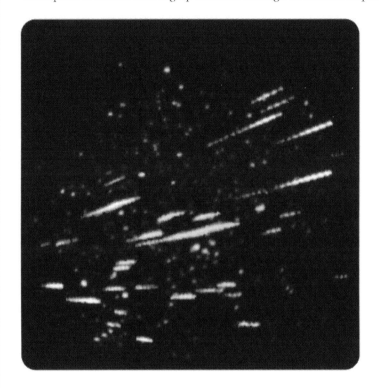

Meteors burning up as they fall through Earth's atmosphere.

Meteoroids

Before these small pieces of matter enter Earth's atmosphere, they are called meteoroids. Meteoroids are as large as boulders or as small as tiny sand grains. Larger objects are called asteroids; smaller objects are interplanetary dust. Meteoroids sometimes cluster together in long trails. They are the debris left behind by comets. When Earth passes through a comet trail, there is a meteor shower. During a meteor shower, there are many more meteors than normal for a night or two.

Meteorites

A meteoroid is dragged towards Earth by gravity and enters the atmosphere. Friction with the atmosphere heats the object quickly, so it starts to vaporize. As it flies through the atmosphere, it leaves a trail of glowing gases. The object is now a meteor. Most meteors vaporize in the atmosphere. They never reach Earth's surface. Large meteoroids may not burn up entirely in the atmosphere. A small core may remain and hit the Earth's surface. This is called a meteorite.

Meteorites provide clues about our solar system. Many were formed in the early solar system (the Figure below). Some are from asteroids that have split apart. A few are rocks from nearby bodies like Mars. For this to happen, an asteroid smashed into Mars and sent up debris. A bit of the debris entered Earth's atmosphere as a meteor.

The Mars Rover, Opportunity, found a metal meteorite on the Red Planet.

COMETS

Comets are small, icy objects that orbit the Sun. Comets have highly elliptical orbits. Their orbits carry them from close to the Sun to the solar system's outer edges. When a comet gets close to the Sun, its outer layers of ice melt and evaporate. The vaporized gas and dust forms an atmosphere around the comet. This atmosphere is called a coma. Radiation and particles streaming from the Sun push some of this gas and dust into a long tail. A comet's tail always points away from the Sun, no matter which way the comet is moving. Why do you think that is? The Figure below shows Comet Hale-Bopp, which shone brightly for several months in 1997.

Gases in the coma and tail of a comet reflect light from the Sun. Comets are very hard to see except when they have comas and tails. That is why they appear only when they are near the Sun. They disappear again as they move back to the outer solar system.
The time between one visit from a comet and the next is called the comet's period. The first comet whose period was known was Halley's Comet. Its period is 75 years. Halley's Comet last traveled through the inner solar system in 1986. The comet will appear again in 2061. Who will look up at it?

Where Comets Come From

Some comets have periods of 200 years or less. They are called short period comets. Short period comets are from a region beyond the orbit of Neptune called the Kuiper Belt. Kuiper is pronounced "KI-per," rhyming with "viper." The Kuiper Belt is home to comets, asteroids, and at least two dwarf planets.

Some comets have periods of thousands or even millions of years. Most long-period comets come from a very distant region of the solar system. This region is called the Oort cloud. The Oort cloud is about 50,000–100,000 times the distance from the Sun to Earth. Comets carry materials in from the outer solar system. Comets may have brought water into the early Earth. Other substances could also have come from comets.

DWARF PLANETS

For several decades, Pluto was a planet. But new solar system objects were discovered that were just as planet-like as Pluto. Astronomers figured out that they were like planets except for one thing. These objects had not cleared their orbits of smaller objects. They didn't have enough gravity to do so. Astronomers made a category called dwarf planets. There are five dwarf planets in our solar system: Ceres, Pluto, Makemake, Haumea and Eris.

Pluto

For decades Pluto was a planet. But even then, scientists knew it was an unusual planet. The other outer planets are all gas giants. Pluto is small, icy and rocky. With a diameter of about 2400 kilometers, it has only about 1/5 the mass of Earth's Moon. The other planets orbit in a plane. Pluto's orbit is tilted. The shape of the orbit is like a long, narrow ellipse. Pluto's orbit is so elliptical that sometimes it is inside the orbit of Neptune.

Pluto's orbit is in the Kuiper belt. We have discovered more than 200 million Kuiper belt objects. Pluto has 3 moons of its own. The largest, Charon, is big. Some scientists think that Pluto-Charon system is a double dwarf planet (The Figure below). Two smaller moons, Nix and Hydra, were discovered in 2005.

Pluto with its moons: Charon, Nix and Hydra.

LESSON SUMMARY

- Asteroids are irregularly-shaped, rocky bodies that orbit the Sun. Most of them are found in the asteroid belt, between the orbits of Mars and Jupiter.
- Meteoroids are smaller than asteroids, ranging from the size of boulders to the size of sand grains. When meteoroids enter Earth's atmosphere, they vaporize, creating a trail of glowing gas called a meteor. If any of the meteoroid reaches Earth, the remaining object is called a meteorite.
- Comets are small, icy objects that orbit the Sun in very elliptical orbits. When they are close to the Sun, they form comas and tails, which glow and make the comet more visible.
- Short-period comets come from the Kuiper belt, beyond Neptune. Long-period comets come from the very distant Oort cloud.
- Dwarf planets are spherical bodies that orbit the Sun, but that have not cleared their orbit of smaller bodies.

LESSON REVIEW QUESTIONS

RECALL

1. Define each of the following: asteroid, meteoroid, meteorite, meteor, planet, dwarf planet.
2. Which type of asteroid is most likely to hit Earth?

APPLY CONCEPTS

3. What is the asteroid belt? Why are there so many asteroids orbiting in this location?
4. What damage can an asteroid do when it hits Earth?

INSIDE EARTH

CHAPTER 2

Standard 2: Students will understand Earth's internal structure and the dynamic nature of the tectonic plates that form its surface.

STANDARD 2, OBJECTIVE 1: EVALUATE THE SOURCE OF EARTH'S INTERNAL HEAT AND THE EVIDENCE OF EARTH'S INTERNAL STRUCTURE.

Earth's Internal Heat

If you think about a volcano, you know Earth must be hot inside. The heat inside Earth moves continents, builds mountains and causes earthquakes. Where does all this heat inside Earth come from?

Earth was hot when it formed. A lot of Earth's heat is leftover from when our planet formed, four-and-a-half billion years ago. Earth is thought to have arisen from a cloud of gas and dust in space. Solid particles, called "planetesimals" condensed out of the cloud. They're thought to have stuck together and created the early Earth. Bombarding planetesimals heated Earth to a molten state. So Earth started out with a lot of heat.

Earth makes some of its own heat. Earth is cooling now – but very, very slowly. Earth is close to a steady temperature state. Over the past several billion years, it might have cooled a couple of hundred degrees. Earth keeps a nearly steady temperature, because it makes heat in its interior.

In other words, Earth has been losing heat since it formed, billions of years ago. But it's producing almost as much heat as it is losing. The process by which Earth makes heat is called radioactive decay. It involves the disintegration of natural radioactive elements inside Earth – like uranium, for example. Uranium is a special kind of element because when it decays, heat is produced. It's this heat that keeps Earth from cooling off completely.

Many of the rocks in Earth's crust and interior undergo this process of radioactive decay. This process produces subatomic particles that zip away, and later collide with surrounding material inside the Earth. Their energy of motion is converted to heat.

Without this process of radioactive decay, there would be fewer volcanoes and earthquakes – and less building of Earth's vast mountain ranges.
(1a text from http://earthsky.org/earth/what-is-the-source-of-the-heat-in-the-earths-interior)

Exploring Earth's Interior

How do scientists know what is inside the Earth? We don't have direct evidence! Rocks yield some clues, but they only reveal information about the outer crust. In rare instances, a mineral, such as a diamond, comes to the surface from deeper down in the crust or the mantle. To learn about Earth's interior, scientists use energy to "see" the different layers of the Earth, just like doctors can use an MRI, CT scan, or x-ray to see inside our bodies.

Seismic Waves

One ingenious way scientists learn about Earth's interior is by looking at how energy travels from the point of an earthquake. These are seismic waves (Figure below). Seismic waves travel outward in all directions from where the ground breaks at an earthquake. These waves are picked up by seismographs around the world. Two types of seismic waves are most useful for learning about Earth's interior.

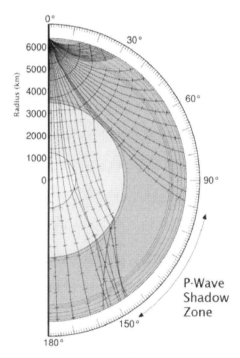

How P-waves travel through Earth's interior.

- P-waves (primary waves) are fastest, traveling at about 6 to 7 kilometers (about 4 miles) per second, so they arrive first at the seismometer. P-waves move in a compression/expansion type motion, squeezing and unsqueezing earth materials as they travel. This produces a change in volume for the material. P-waves bend slightly when they travel from one layer into another. Seismic waves move faster through denser or more rigid material. As P-waves encounter the liquid outer core, which is less rigid than the mantle, they slow down. This makes the P-waves arrive later and further away than would be expected. The result is a P-wave shadow zone. No P-waves are picked up at seismographs 104o to 140o from the earthquakes focus.

- S-waves (secondary waves) are about half as fast as P-waves, traveling at about 3.5 km (2 miles) per second, and arrive second at seismographs. S-waves move in an up and down motion perpendicular to the direction of wave travel. This produces a change in shape for the earth materials they move through. Only solids resist a change in shape, so S-waves are only able to propagate through solids. S-waves cannot travel through liquid.

By tracking seismic waves, scientists have learned what makes up the planet's interior (Figure below).

- P-waves slow down at the mantle core boundary, so we know the outer core is less rigid than the mantle.
- S-waves disappear at the mantle core boundary, so the outer core is liquid.

This animation shows a seismic wave shadow zone:
http://earthquake.usgs.gov/learn/animations/animation.php?flash_title=Shadow+Zone&flash_file=shadowzone&flash_width=220&flash_height=320.

Letters describe the path of an individual P-wave or S-wave. Waves traveling through the core take on the letter K.

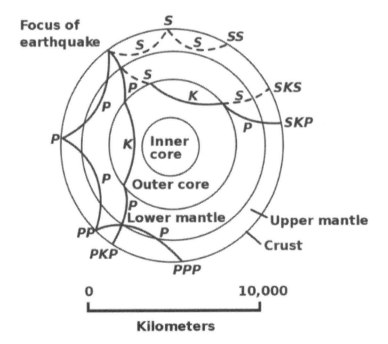

Other Clues about Earth's Interior

- Earth's overall density is higher than the density of crustal rocks, so the core must be made of something dense, like metal.
- Since Earth has a magnetic field, there must be metal within the planet. Iron and nickel are both magnetic.
- Meteorites are the remains of the material that formed the early solar system and are thought to be similar to material in Earth's interior (Figure below).

This meteorite contains silica minerals and iron-nickel. The material is like the boundary between Earth's core and mantle. The meteorite is 4.2 billion years old.

THE EARTH'S LAYERS

The layers scientists recognize are pictured below.

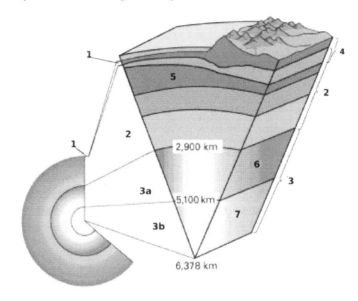

A cross section of Earth showing the following layers: (1) crust (2) mantle (3a) outer core (3b) inner core (4) lithosphere (5) asthenosphere (6) outer core (7) inner core.

Core, mantle, and crust are divisions based on composition:

- The crust is less than 1% of Earth by mass. The oceanic crust is mafic (minerals with high levels of ferromagnesian), while continental crust is often more felsic (minerals that are primarily made of feldspars and quartz) rock.
- The mantle is hot, ultramafic rock. It represents about 68% of Earth's mass.
- The core is mostly iron metal. The core makes up about 31% of the Earth.

Lithosphere and asthenosphere are divisions based on mechanical properties:

- The lithosphere is composed of both the crust and the portion of the upper mantle that behaves as a brittle, rigid solid.
- The asthenosphere is partially molten upper mantle material that behaves plastically and can flow.
- The mesosphere refers to the mantle in the region under the lithosphere, and the asthenosphere, but above the outer core. The difference between mesosphere and asthenosphere is likely due to density and rigidity differences, that is, physical factors, and not to any difference in chemical composition.

This animation shows the layers by composition and by mechanical properties:
http://earthguide.ucsd.edu/eoc/teachers/t_tectonics/p_layers.html.

Crust and Lithosphere

Earth's outer surface is its crust; a cold, thin, brittle outer shell made of rock. The crust is very thin, relative to the radius of the planet. There are two very different types of crust, each with its own distinctive physical and chemical properties, which are summarized in Table below.

Crust	Thickness	Density	Composition	Rock types
Oceanic	5-12 km (3-8 mi)	3.0 g/cm3	Mafic	Basalt and gabbro
Continental	Avg. 35 km (22 mi)	2.7 g/cm3	Felsic	All types

Oceanic crust is composed of mafic magma that erupts on the seafloor to create basalt lava flows or cools deeper down to create the intrusive igneous rock gabbro (Figure below).

Gabbro from ocean crust

The gabbro is deformed because of intense faulting at the eruption site.

Sediments, primarily muds and the shells of tiny sea creatures, coat the seafloor. Sediment is thickest near the shore where it comes off the continents in rivers and on wind currents.

Continental crust is made up of many different types of igneous, metamorphic, and sedimentary rocks. The average composition is granite, which is much less dense than the mafic rocks of the oceanic crust (Figure below). Because it is thick and has relatively low density, continental crust rises higher on the mantle than oceanic crust, which sinks into the mantle to form basins. When filled with water, these basins form the planet's oceans.

This granite from Missouri is more than 1 billion years old.

The lithosphere is the outermost mechanical layer, which behaves as a brittle, rigid solid. The lithosphere is about 100 kilometers thick. Look at the figure above. Can you find where the crust and the lithosphere are located? How are they different from each other? The definition of the lithosphere is based on how earth materials behave, so it includes the crust and the uppermost mantle, which are both brittle. Since it is rigid and brittle, when stresses act on the lithosphere, it breaks. This is what we experience as an earthquake.

Mantle

The two most important things about the mantle are: (1) it is made of solid rock, and (2) it is hot. Scientists know that the mantle is made of rock based on evidence from seismic waves, heat flow, and meteorites. The properties fit the ultramafic rock peridotite, which is made of the iron- and magnesium-rich silicate minerals (Figure below). Peridotite is rarely found at Earth's surface.

Peridotite is formed of crystals of olivine (green) and pyroxene (black).

Scientists know that the mantle is extremely hot because of the heat flowing outward from it and because of its physical properties.

Heat flows in two different ways within the Earth:

1. Conduction: Heat is transferred through rapid collisions of atoms, which can only happen if the material is solid. Heat flows from warmer to cooler places until all are the same temperature. The mantle is hot mostly because of heat conducted from the core.

2. Convection: If a material is able to move, even if it moves very slowly, convection currents can form.

Convection in the mantle is the same as convection in a pot of water on a stove. Convection currents within Earth's mantle form as material near the core heats up. As the core heats the bottom layer of mantle material, particles move more rapidly, decreasing its density and causing it to rise. The rising material begins the convection current. When the warm material reaches the surface, it spreads horizontally. The material cools because it is no longer near the core. It eventually becomes cool and dense enough to sink back down into the mantle. At the bottom of the mantle, the material travels horizontally and is heated by the core. It reaches the location where warm mantle material rises, and the mantle convection cell is complete (Figure below).

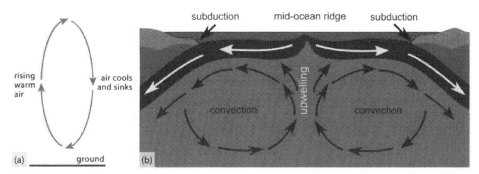

In a convection cell, warm material rises and cool material sinks. In mantle convection, the heat source is the core.

Diagram of convection within Earth's mantle.

Core

At the planet's center lies a dense metallic core. Scientists know that the core is metal because:

- The density of Earth's surface layers is much less than the overall density of the planet, as calculated from the planet's rotation. If the surface layers are less dense than average, then the interior must be denser than average. Calculations indicate that the core is about 85% iron metal with nickel metal making up much of the remaining 15%.

- Metallic meteorites are thought to be representative of the core. The 85% iron/15% nickel calculation above is also seen in metallic meteorites (Figure below).

An iron meteorite is the closest thing to the Earth's core that we can hold in our hands.

If Earth's core were not metal, the planet would not have a magnetic field. Metals such as iron are magnetic, but rock, which makes up the mantle and crust, is not.

Scientists know that the outer core is liquid and the inner core is solid because:

1. S-waves stop at the inner core.
2. The strong magnetic field is caused by convection in the liquid outer core. Convection currents in the outer core are due to heat from the even hotter inner core.

The heat that keeps the outer core from solidifying is produced by the breakdown of radioactive elements in the inner core.

LESSON SUMMARY

Earth is made of three layers: the crust, mantle, and core.
The brittle crust and uppermost mantle are together called the lithosphere.
Beneath the lithosphere, the mantle is solid rock that can flow, or behave plastically.
The hot core warms the base of the mantle, which causes mantle convection.

REVIEW QUESTIONS

1. What are the two main ways that scientists learn about Earth's interior and what do these two things indicate?
2. What is the difference between crust and lithosphere? Include in your answer both where they are located and what their properties are.
3. How do the differences between oceanic and continental crust lead to the presence of ocean basins and continents?
4. What types of rock make up the oceanic crust and how do they form?
5. What types of rock make up the continental crust?
6. How do scientists know about the liquid outer core? How do scientists know that the outer core is liquid?
7. Describe the properties of each of these parts of the Earth's interior: lithosphere, mantle, and core. What are they made of? How hot are they? What are their physical properties?
8. When you put your hand above a pan filled with boiling water, does your hand warm up because of convection or conduction? If you touch the pan, does your hand warm up because of convection or conduction? Based on your answers, which type of heat transfer moves heat more easily and efficiently?

Points to Consider

9. Oceanic crust is thinner and denser than continental crust. All crust sits atop the mantle. What might Earth be like if this were not true?
10. If sediments fall onto the seafloor over time, what can sediment thickness tell scientists about the age of the seafloor in different regions?
11. How might convection cells in the mantle affect the movement of solid crust on the planet's surface?

STANDARD 2, OBJECTIVE 2: DESCRIBE THE DEVELOPMENT OF THE CURRENT THEORY OF PLATE TECTONICS AND THE EVIDENCE THAT SUPPORTS THIS THEORY.

'Doesn't the east coast of South America fit exactly against the west coast of Africa, as if they had once been joined? This is an idea I'll have to pursue.' - Alfred Wegener said to his future wife, in December, 1910. We can't really get into Alfred Wegener's head, but we can imagine that he started his investigations by trying to answer this question: Why do the continents of Africa and South America appear to fit together so well? Is it a geometric coincidence that they do, or is there some geological reason?

Wegener's Idea

Alfred Wegener, born in 1880, was a meteorologist and explorer. In 1911, Wegener found a scientific paper that listed identical plant and animal fossils on opposite sides of the Atlantic Ocean. Intrigued, he then searched for and found other cases of identical fossils on opposite sides of oceans. The explanation put out by the scientists of the day was that land bridges had once stretched between these continents. Instead, Wegener pondered the way Africa and South America appeared to fit together like puzzle pieces. Other scientists had suggested that Africa and South America had once been joined, but Wegener was the idea's greatest supporter. Wegener obtained a tremendous amount of evidence to support his hypothesis that the continents had once been joined. Imagine that you're Wegener's colleague. What sort of evidence would you look for to see if the continents had actually been joined and had moved apart?

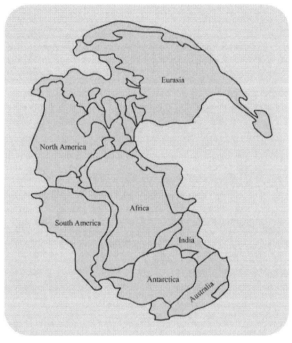

Wegener's Evidence

Here is the main evidence that Wegener and his supporters collected for the continental drift hypothesis:

1. The continents appear to fit together.
2. Ancient fossils of the same species of extinct plants and animals are found in rocks of the same age but are on continents that are now widely separated (See Figure 2.2a Image 2). Wegener proposed that the organisms had lived side by side, but that the lands had moved apart after they were dead and fossilized. His critics suggested that the organisms moved over long-gone land bridges, but Wegener thought that the organisms could not have been able to travel across the oceans.

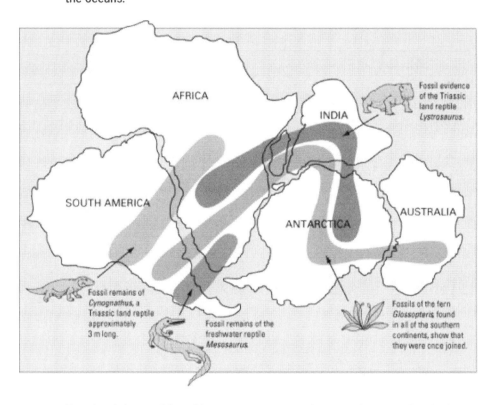

- Fossils of the seed fern Glossopteris were too heavy to be carried so far by wind.
- Mesosaurus was a swimming reptile, but could only swim in fresh water.
- Cynognathus and Lystrosaurus were land reptiles and were unable to swim.

3. Identical rocks, of the same type and age, are found on both sides of the Atlantic Ocean. Wegener said the rocks had formed side by side and that the land had since moved apart.

4. Mountain ranges with the same rock types, structures, and ages are now on opposite sides of the Atlantic Ocean. The Appalachians of the eastern United States and Canada, for example, are just like mountain ranges in eastern Greenland, Ireland, Great Britain, and Norway (See Figure 2.2a Image 3). Wegener concluded that they formed as a single mountain range that was separated as the continents drifted.

Appalachian Mountain range

Eastern Greenland mountain range

5. Grooves and rock deposits left by ancient glaciers are found today on different continents very close to the equator. This would indicate that the glaciers either formed in the middle of the ocean and/or covered most of the Earth. Today, glaciers only form on land and nearer the poles. Wegener thought that the glaciers were centered over the southern land mass close to the South Pole and the continents moved to their present positions later on.

6. Coral reefs and coal-forming swamps are found in tropical and subtropical environments, but ancient coal seams and coral reefs are found in locations where it is much too cold today. Wegener suggested that these creatures were alive in warm climate zones and that the fossils and coal later drifted to new locations on the continents. An animation showing that Earth's climate belts remain in roughly the same position while the continents move is seen here: http://www.scotese.com/paleocli.htm.

7. Wegener thought that mountains formed as continents ran into each other. This got around the problem of the leading hypothesis of the day, which was that Earth had been a molten ball that bulked up in spots as it cooled (the problem with this idea was that the mountains should all be the same age and they were known not to be).

Problems with his Theory

Even with many forms of evidence that the continents had once fit together and had since moved apart into their present locations, the scientific community at the time could not fully accept his theory. The biggest reason for the rejection of his evidence was that Wegener could not provide an explanation for how something as large as continents could move or by which force they could collide into one another. Wegener incorrectly proposed that the continents were plowing through the ocean floor, but there was no obvious mechanism for how this could be accomplished. Because of this lack of an explanation, Alfred Wegener's hypothesis of continental drift was not widely accepted in his day. However, modern discoveries in plate techtonic theory have greatly led to a further understanding and wider acceptance of his theory.

Magnetic Polarity Evidence

The next breakthrough in the development of the theory of plate tectonics came two decades after Wegener's death. Magnetite crystals are shaped like a tiny bar magnet. As basalt lava cools, the magnetite crystals line up in the magnetic field like tiny magnets. When the lava is completely cooled, the crystals point in the direction of magnetic north pole at the time they form. How do you expect this would help scientists see whether continents had moved or not?

You have just learned of a new tool that may help you. A magnetometer is a device capable of measuring the magnetic field intensity. This allows you to look at the magnetic properties of rocks in many locations, including basalt along the ocean floor.

What causes the Magnetic Stripes on the seafloor?

This pattern of magnetic stripes could represent what scientists see on the seafloor. Note that the stripes are symmetrical about the central dusky purple stripe. In the oceans, magnetic stripes are symmetrical about a mid-ocean ridge axis. What could cause this? What could it possibly mean?

Seafloor Magnetism

During world war II, ships towed magnetometers in the ocean in order to find enemy submarines. They observed that the magnetic field strength changed from normal to reversed polarity as they sailed across the ocean. When scientists plotted the points of normal and reversed polarity on a seafloor map they made an astonishing discovery: the normal and reversed magnetic polarity of seafloor basalts creates a pattern:

- Stripes of normal polarity and reversed polarity alternate across the ocean bottom.
- Stripes form mirror images on either side of the mid-ocean ridges.
- Stripes end abruptly at the edges of continents, sometimes at a deep sea trench.

Seafloor Age

By combining magnetic polarity data from rocks on land and on the seafloor with radiometric age dating and fossil ages, scientists came up with a time scale for the magnetic reversals. The scientists noticed that the rocks got older with distance from the mid-ocean ridges. The youngest rocks were located at the ridge crest and the oldest rocks were located the farthest away, next to continents. Scientists also noticed that the characteristics of the rocks and sediments changed with distance from the ridge axis as seen in the Table below.

	Rock Ages	Sediment Thicknesses	Crust Thicknesses	Heat Flow
At mid-ocean ridge	Youngest	None	Thinnest	Hottest
With distance from mid-ocean ridge	Becomes older	Becomes thicker	Becomes thicker	Becomes cooler

Data From the Sea Floor

Away from the ridge crest, sediment becomes older and thicker, and the seafloor becomes thicker. Heat flow, which indicates that ocean crust is highest at the mid-ocean ridge.

The oldest seafloor is near the edges of continents or deep sea trenches and is less than 180 million years old (See Figure 2.3). Since the oldest ocean crust is so much younger than the oldest continental crust, scientists realized that something was happening to the older seafloor.

How can you explain the observations that scientists have made in the oceans? Why is rock younger at the ridge and oldest at the farthest points from the ridge? The scientists suggested that seafloor was being created at the ridge. Since the planet is not getting larger, they suggested that it is destroyed in a relatively short amount of geologic time. This 65 minute video explains "The Role of Paleomagnetism in the Evolution of Plate Tectonic Theory":
http://online.wr.usgs.gov/calendar/2004/jul04.html.

The Development of the Plate Tectonics Theory

Harry Hess was a geology professor and a naval officer who commanded an attack transport ship during WWII. Like other ships, Hess's ship had echo sounders that mapped the seafloor. Hess discovered hundreds of flat-topped mountains in the Pacific that he gave the name guyot. He puzzled at what could have formed mountains that appeared to be eroded at the top but were more than a mile beneath the sea surface. Hess also noticed trenches that were as much as 7 miles deep.

Meanwhile, other scientists like Bruce Heezen discovered the underwater mountain range they called the Great Global Rift. Although the rift was mostly in the deep sea, it occasionally came close to land. These scientists thought the rift was a set of breaks in Earth's crust. The final piece that was needed was the work of Vine and Matthews, who had discovered the bands of alternating magnetic polarity in the seafloor symmetrically about the rift.

SEAFLOOR SPREADING

Seafloor Bathymetry

During World War II, battleships and submarines carried echo sounders to locate enemy submarines (Figure below). Echo sounders produce sound waves that travel outward in all directions, bounce off the nearest object, and then return to the ship. By knowing the speed of sound in seawater, scientists calculate the distance to the object based on the time it takes for the wave to make a round-trip. During the war, most of the sound waves ricocheted off the ocean bottom.

This echo sounder has many beams and creates a three dimensional map of the seafloor. Early echo sounders had a single beam and created a line of depth measurements.

This animation shows how sound waves are used to create pictures of the sea floor and ocean crust:
http://earthguide.ucsd.edu/eoc/teachers/t_tectonics/p_sonar.html.

After the war, scientists pieced together the ocean depths to produce bathymetric maps, which reveal the features of the ocean floor as if the water were taken away. Even scientist were amazed that the seafloor was not completely flat (Figure right).

A modern map of the southeastern Pacific and Atlantic Oceans.

The major features of the ocean basins and their colors on the map in Figure right include:

- mid-ocean ridges: rise up high above the deep seafloor as a long chain of mountains; e.g. the light blue gash in middle of Atlantic Ocean.
- deep sea trenches: found at the edges of continents or in the sea near chains of active volcanoes; e.g. the very deepest blue, off of western South America.
- abyssal plains: flat areas, although many are dotted with volcanic mountains; e.g. consistent blue off of southeastern South America.

When they first observed these bathymetric maps, scientists wondered what had formed these features.

Seafloor Magnetism

Sometimes -- no one really knows why -- the magnetic poles switch positions. North becomes south and south becomes north.

- Normal polarity: north and south poles are aligned as they are now.
- Reversed polarity: north and south poles are in the opposite position.

During WWII, magnetometers attached to ships to search for submarines located an astonishing feature: the normal and reversed magnetic polarity of seafloor basalts creates a pattern.

- Stripes of normal polarity and reversed polarity alternate across the ocean bottom.
- Stripes form mirror images on either side of the mid-ocean ridges (Figure below).
- Stripes end abruptly at the edges of continents, sometimes at a deep sea trench (Figure below).

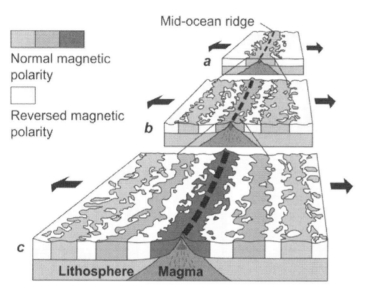

Magnetic polarity is normal at the ridge crest but reversed in symmetrical patterns away from the ridge center. This normal and reversed pattern continues across the seafloor.

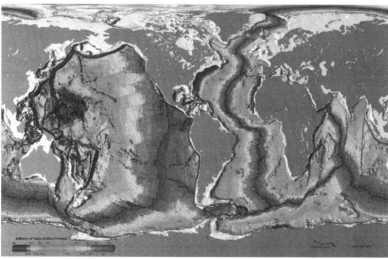

Seafloor is youngest at the mid-ocean ridges and becomes progressively older with distance from the ridge.

The characteristics of the rocks and sediments change with distance from the ridge axis as seen in the Table below.

	Rock ages	Sediment thickness	Crust thickness	Heat flow
At ridge axis	youngest	none	thinnest	hottest
With distance from axis	becomes older	becomes thicker	becomes thicker	becomes cooler

A map of sediment thickness is found here:
http://earthguide.ucsd.edu/eoc/teachers/t_tectonics/p_sedimentthickness.html.

The oldest seafloor is near the edges of continents or deep sea trenches and is less than 180 million years old (Figure above). Since the oldest ocean crust is so much younger than the oldest continental crust, scientists realized that seafloor was being destroyed in a relatively short time.

This 65 minute video explains "The Role of Paleomagnetism in the Evolution of Plate Tectonic Theory":
http://online.wr.usgs.gov/calendar/2004/jul04.html

The Seafloor Spreading Hypothesis
Scientists brought these observations together in the early 1960s to create the seafloor spreading hypothesis. In this hypothesis, hot buoyant mantle rises up a mid-ocean ridge, causing the ridge to rise upward (Figure right).

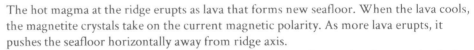

Magma at the mid-ocean ridge creates new seafloor.

The hot magma at the ridge erupts as lava that forms new seafloor. When the lava cools, the magnetite crystals take on the current magnetic polarity. As more lava erupts, it pushes the seafloor horizontally away from ridge axis.

These animations show the creation of magnetic stripes of normal and reversed polarity at a mid-ocean ridge:
http://www.nature.nps.gov/GEOLOGY/usgsnps/animate/A49.gif;http://www.nature.nps.gov/GEOLOGY/usgsnps/animate/A55.gif.

The magnetic stripes continue across the seafloor.
- As oceanic crust forms and spreads, moving away from the ridge crest, it pushes the continent away from the ridge axis.
- If the oceanic crust reaches a deep sea trench, it sinks into the trench and is lost into the mantle.
- The oldest crust is coldest and lies deepest in the ocean because it is less buoyant than the hot new crust.

The Mechanism for Continental Drift

Seafloor spreading is the mechanism for Wegener's drifting continents. Convection currents within the mantle take the continents on a conveyor-belt ride of oceanic crust that, over millions of years, takes them around the planet's surface. The spreading plate takes along any continent that rides on it.

Seafloor spreading is the topic of this Discovery Education video:
http://video.yahoo.com/watch/1595570/5390151.
The history of the seafloor spreading hypothesis and the evidence that was collected to develop it are the subject of this video:
http://www.youtube.com/watch?v=6CsTTmvX6mc&feature=rec-LGOUT-exp_fresh+div-1r-2 (8:05).

The Theory of Plate Tectonics—What is a Plate?

During the 1950s and early 1960s, scientists set up seismograph networks to see if enemy nations were testing atomic bombs. These seismographs also recorded all of the earthquakes around the planet. The seismic records were used to locate an earthquake's epicenter, the point on Earth's surface directly above the place where the earthquake occurs.

Why is this relevant? It turns out that earthquake epicenters outline the plates. This is because earthquakes occur everywhere plates come into contact with each other. In addition to this, a vast number of volcanoes from around the world are also located where plates meet. With this evidence and the combined evidences about Sea Floor Spreading, magnetic striping of the ocean floor, and more, the answer to what could cause the Continents to Drift apart became real.

The Plate Tectonics theory provides the answers to the two questions that Alfred Wegener could not explain. 1) what causes plates to move, and what force could cause this to happen? Today, our general understanding about the Plate Tectonic Theory is that the Earth is divided into several crustal plates composed of oceanic lithosphere and thicker continental lithosphere, each topped by its own kind of crust. Tectonic plates are able to move because the Earth's lithosphere has a higher strength and lower density than the underlying asthenosphere. Along convergent boundaries, subduction carries plates into the mantle; the material lost is roughly balanced by the formation of new (oceanic) crust along mid-ocean ridges by seafloor spreading. In this way, the total surface of the globe remains the same. Tectonic plates are able to move because the Earth's lithosphere has a higher strength and lower density than the underlying asthenosphere. Plate movement is thought to be driven by a combination of the motion of the seafloor away from the mid-ocean ridges (due to variations in topography and density of the crust, which result in differences in gravitational forces) and drag, downward suction, at the subduction zones.

Mantle Plumes & Hot Spots

(This section is adapted from *http://pubs.usgs.gov/gip/dynamic/hotspots.html*)

The vast majority of earthquakes and volcanic eruptions occur near plate boundaries, but there are some exceptions. For example, the Hawaiian Islands, which are entirely of volcanic origin, have formed in the middle of the Pacific Ocean more than 3,200 km from the nearest plate boundary. How do the Hawaiian Islands and other volcanoes that form in the interior of plates fit into the plate-tectonics picture?

In 1963, J. Tuzo Wilson, the Canadian geophysicist who discovered transform faults, came up with an ingenious idea that became known as the "hot spot" theory. Wilson noted that in certain locations around the world, such as Hawaii, volcanism has been active for very long periods of time. This could only happen, he reasoned, if relatively small, long-lasting, and exceptionally hot regions -- called hot spots -- existed below the plates that would provide localized sources of high heat energy (thermal plumes) to sustain volcanism. Specifically, Wilson hypothesized that the distinctive linear shape of the Hawaiian Island-Emperor Seamounts chain resulted from the Pacific Plate moving over a deep, stationary hotspot in the mantle, located beneath the present-day position of the Island of Hawaii. Heat from this hotspot produced a persistent source of magma by partly melting the overriding Pacific Plate. The magma, which is lighter than the surrounding solid rock, then rises through the mantle and crust to erupt onto the seafloor, forming an active seamount. Over time, countless eruptions cause the seamount to grow until it finally emerges above sea level to form an island volcano. Wilson suggested that continuing plate movement eventually carries the island beyond the hotspot, cutting it off from the magma source, and volcanism ceases. As one island volcano becomes extinct, another develops over the hotspot, and the cycle is repeated. See Figure below. This process of volcano growth and death, over many millions of years, has left a long trail of volcanic islands and seamounts across the Pacific Ocean floor.

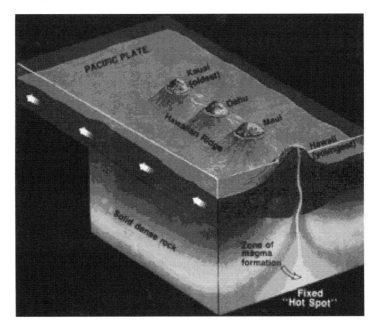

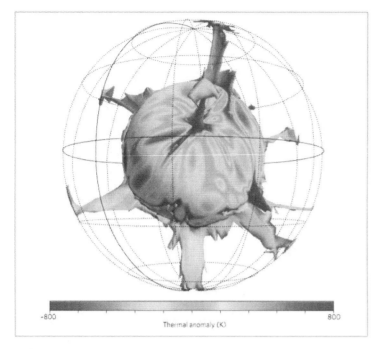

Other known hot spots from around the world can be found in the figure below.

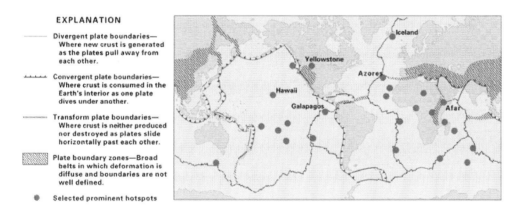

Earth's Tectonic Plates

Seafloor and continents move around on Earth's surface, but what is actually moving? What portion of the Earth makes up the "plates" in plate tectonics? This question was also answered because of technology developed during war times - in this case, the Cold War. The plates are made up of the lithosphere.

During the 1950s and early 1960s, scientists set up seismograph networks to see if enemy nations were testing atomic bombs. These seismographs also recorded all of the earthquakes around the planet. The seismic records could be used to locate an earthquake's epicenter, the point on Earth's surface directly above the place where the earthquake occurs.

Earthquake epicenters outline the plates. Mid-ocean ridges, trenches, and large faults mark the edges of the plates, and this is where earthquakes occur (Figure below).

Preliminary Determination of Epicenters
358,214 Events, 1963 - 1998

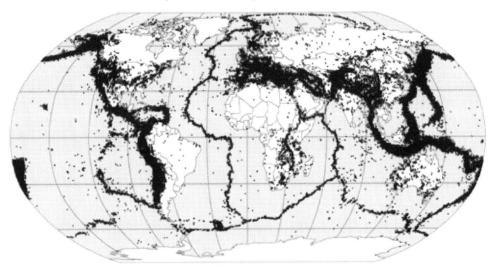

Earthquakes outline the plates.

The lithosphere is divided into a dozen major and several minor plates (Figurebelow). The plates' edges can be drawn by connecting the dots that mark earthquakes' epicenters. A single plate can be made of all oceanic lithosphere or all continental lithosphere, but nearly all plates are made of a combination of both.

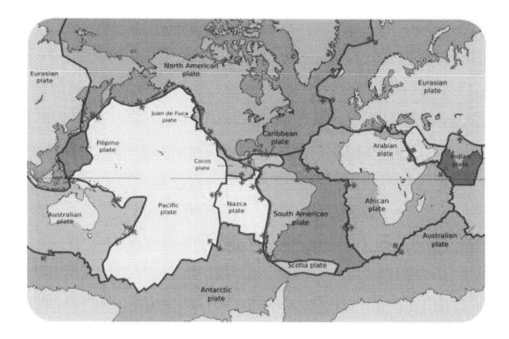

The lithospheric plates and their names are shown in the figure above. The arrows show whether the plates are moving apart, moving together, or sliding past each other.

Movement of the plates over Earth's surface is termed plate tectonics. Plates move at a rate of a few centimeters a year, about the same rate fingernails grow.

Volcanoes

During a volcano, the heat energy is transferred through lava to the Earth's surface. The magma may come up to the surface as maglavama bringing heat energy with it. The volcanoes which erupt on the island of Hawaii are an example of this transfer of heat energy. Notice, the lava is very hot as it comes up to the surface. The lava immediately begins to cool. As the heat escapes, the lava hardens to dark black rock.

Magma which becomes trapped below the surface can build up pressure that must be released as mechanical energy. An example of this release of mechanical energy was the eruption of Mt. Saint Helens in Washington State. As the heat energy in the magma built up below the surface of the mountain, the pressure increased. This pressure was released in a gigantic explosion which blew off the top of the mountain.

Earthquakes

The transfer of earthquake energy happens in the form of waves. These waves can happen in a couple of different ways.

The energy from an earthquake arrives in three distinct waves. The fastest and therefore the first to arrive was named the Primary wave or p-wave. The second to arrive was named the secondary wave or s-wave. The slowest and last to arrive was named the surface wave.

P-wave: P-waves are a form of longitudinal waves. These waves vibrate in a direction parallel to the direction in which the energy is transferred. For example, in an east moving p-wave objects vibrate in an east-west direction. This is the type of wave demonstrated in the first two videos above.

S-wave: S-waves are a form of transverse waves. These waves vibrate in a direction perpendicular to the direction in which the energy is transferred. For example, in an east moving s-wave, objects vibrate in a north-south direction. This is more destructive than the vibrations in a p-wave. This is the type of wave demonstrated in the third video above.

Surface Wave: Also known as a Love wave, the surface wave is much slower than the p-wave or s-wave. A surface wave is a combination of a transverse and a longitudinal wave in which the particles vibrate both perpendicularly and parallel to the direction of energy transfer. An object struck by a surface wave would vibrate both north-south and east-west. The result is that the objects move in a circle. This is the most destructive of the three types of wave. A surface wave is similar to the ripples you see when an object is dropped into a body of water. Observe a QuickTime video of this type of wave. (click the back button of your browser to return to this page.) In this next video, notice the motion of the ball floating in the water. If you watch closely, you can see the circular motion. Observe a QuickTime video of this circular motion. (click the back button of your browser to return to this page.)
(info from http://utahscience.oremjr.alpine.k12.ut.us/sciber08/8th/geology/html/wavenrgy.htm)

SUMMARY

- Seafloor spreading brought together the mantle convection idea of Holmes, the continental drift idea of Wegener, new bathymetric and magnetic data from the seafloor, and made a coherent single idea.
- Harry Hess called his idea "an essay in geopoetry," possibly because so many ideas fit together so well, or more likely because at the time he didn't have all the seafloor data he needed for evidence.
- Seafloor spreading is the mechanism for the drifting continents.
- Data from magnetometers dragged behind ships looking for enemy submarines in WWII discovered amazing magnetic patterns on the seafloor.
- Rocks of normal and reversed polarity are found in stripes symmetrically about the mid-ocean ridge axis.
- The age of seafloor rocks increases from the ridge crest to rocks the farthest from the ridges. Still, the rocks of the ocean basins are much younger than most of the rocks of the continents.
- Alfred Wegener did some background reading and made an observation. Wegener then asked an important question and set about to answer it. He collected a great deal of evidence to support his idea. Wegener's evidence included the fit of the continents, the distribution of ancient fossils, the placement of similar rocks and structures on the opposite sides of oceans, and indicators of ancient climate found in locations where those climates do not exist today.

Review
1. How did Wegener become interested in the idea that continents could move?
2. What did he need to do to explore the question and make it into a reasonable hypothesis?
3. How did Wegener use fossil evidence to support his hypothesis?
4. How did Wegener use climate evidence from rocks to support his hypothesis?

Practice (Use this resource to answer the questions that follow.
http://earthguide.ucsd.edu/eoc/teachers/t_tectonics/p_seafloorspreading.html)

1. Where does seafloor spreading occur?
2. What is the average elevation of the ocean ridges?
3. What are the characteristics of the seafloor near these ridges?
4. Explain why a ridge exists.
5. How fast is the spreading occurring?

Review
1. How does the pattern of magnetic stripes give evidence for seafloor spreading?
2. How does the topography of the seafloor give evidence for seafloor spreading?
3. How does seafloor spreading fit into the idea that continents move about on Earth's surface?

STANDARD 2, OBJECTIVE 3: DEMONSTRATE HOW THE MOTION OF TECTONIC PLATES AFFECTS EARTH AND LIVING THINGS.

How Plates Move

- If seafloor spreading drives the plates, what drives seafloor spreading? Picture two convection cells side-by-side in the mantle, similar to the illustration in Figure below.
- Hot mantle from the two adjacent cells rises at the ridge axis, creating new ocean crust.
- The top limb of the convection cell moves horizontally away from the ridge crest, as does the new seafloor.
-
- The outer limbs of the convection cells plunge down into the deeper mantle, dragging oceanic crust as well. This takes place at the deep sea trenches.
- The material sinks to the core and moves horizontally.
- The material heats up and reaches the zone where it rises again.

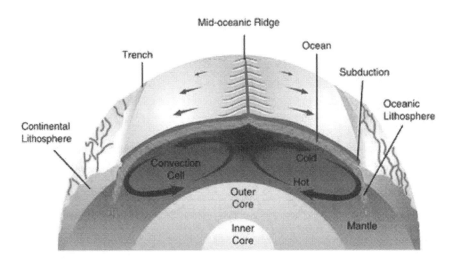

Mantle convection drives plate tectonics. Hot material rises at mid-ocean ridges and sinks at deep sea trenches, which keeps the plates moving along the Earth's surface.

Mantle convection is shown in these animations:
http://www.youtube.com/watch?v=p0dWF_3PYh4
http://earthguide.ucsd.edu/eoc/teachers/t_tectonics/p_convection2.html

Plate Boundaries

Plate boundaries are the edges where two plates meet. Most geologic activities, including volcanoes, earthquakes, and mountain building, take place at plate boundaries. How can two plates move relative to each other?

- **Divergent plate boundaries: the two plates move away from each other.**
- **Convergent plate boundaries: the two plates move towards each other.**
- **Transform plate boundaries: the two plates slip past each other.**

The type of plate boundary and the type of crust found on each side of the boundary determines what sort of geologic activity will be found there.

Divergent Plate Boundaries

Plates move apart at mid-ocean ridges where new seafloor forms. Between the two plates is a rift valley. Lava flows at the surface cool rapidly to become basalt, but deeper in the crust, magma cools more slowly to form gabbro. So the entire ridge system is made up of igneous rock that is either extrusive or intrusive. Earthquakes are common at mid-ocean ridges since the movement of magma and oceanic crust results in crustal shaking. The vast majority of mid-ocean ridges are located deep below the sea (Figure below).

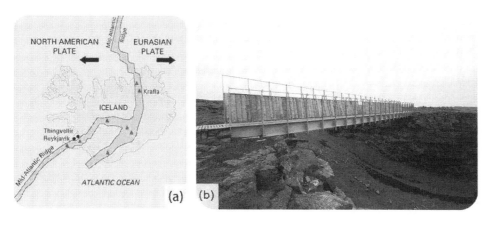

(a) Iceland is the one location where the ridge is located on land: the Mid-Atlantic Ridge separates the North American and Eurasian plates; (b) The rift valley in the Mid-Atlantic Ridge on Iceland.

USGS animation of divergent plate boundary at mid-ocean ridge:

http://earthquake.usgs.gov/learn/animations/animation.php?flash_title=Divergent+Boundary&flash_file=divergent&flash_width=500&flash_height=200.

Divergent plate boundary animation:
http://www.iris.edu/hq/files/programs/education_and_outreach/aotm/11/AOTM_09_01_Divergent_480.mov.

Can divergent plate boundaries occur within a continent? What is the result? In continental rifting (Figure right), magma rises beneath the continent, causing it to become thinner, break, and ultimately split apart. New ocean crust erupts in the void, creating an ocean between continents.

The Arabian, Indian, and African plates are rifting apart, forming the Great Rift Valley in Africa. The Dead Sea fills the rift with seawater.

Convergent Plate Boundaries

When two plates converge, the result depends on the type of lithosphere the plates are made of. No matter what, smashing two enormous slabs of lithosphere together results in magma generation and earthquakes.

Ocean-continent: When oceanic crust converges with continental crust, the denser oceanic plate plunges beneath the continental plate. This process, called subduction, occurs at the oceanic trenches (Figure below). The entire region is known as a subduction zone. Subduction zones have a lot of intense earthquakes and volcanic eruptions. The subducting plate causes melting in the mantle. The magma rises and erupts, creating volcanoes. These coastal volcanic mountains are found in a line above the subducting plate (Figure below). The volcanoes are known as a continental arc.

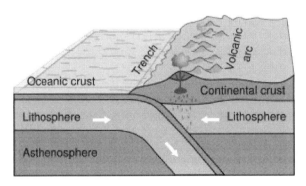

Subduction of an oceanic plate beneath a continental plate causes earthquakes and forms a line of volcanoes known as a continental arc.

The movement of crust and magma causes earthquakes. A map of earthquake epicenters at subduction zones is found here:
http://earthguide.ucsd.edu/eoc/teachers/t_tectonics/p_earthquakessubduction.html.

This animation shows the relationship between subduction of the lithosphere and creation of a volcanic arc:
http://earthguide.ucsd.edu/eoc/teachers/t_tectonics/p_subduction.html.

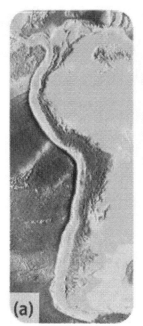

(a) At the trench lining the western margin of South America, the Nazca plate is subducting beneath the South American plate, resulting in the Andes Mountains (brown and red uplands); (b) Convergence has pushed up limestone in the Andes Mountains where volcanoes are common.

The volcanoes of northeastern California—Lassen Peak, Mount Shasta, and Medicine Lake volcano—along with the rest of the Cascade Mountains of the Pacific Northwest are the result of subduction of the Juan de Fuca plate beneath the North American plate (Figure right). The Juan de Fuca plate is created by seafloor spreading just offshore at the Juan de Fuca ridge.

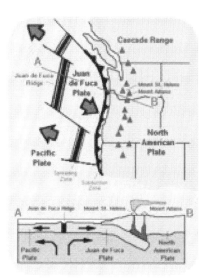

The Cascade Mountains of the Pacific Northwest are a continental arc.

If the magma at a continental arc is felsic, it may be too viscous (thick) to rise through the crust. The magma will cool slowly to form granite or granodiorite. These large bodies of intrusive igneous rocks are called batholiths, which may someday be uplifted to form a mountain range (Figure below).

The Sierra Nevada batholith cooled beneath a volcanic arc roughly 200 million years ago. The rock is well exposed here at Mount Whitney. Similar batholiths are likely forming beneath the Andes and Cascades today.

Ocean-ocean: When two oceanic plates converge, the older, denser plate will subduct into the mantle. An ocean trench marks the location where the plate is pushed down into the mantle. The line of volcanoes that grows on the upper oceanic plate is an island arc. Do you think earthquakes are common in these regions?

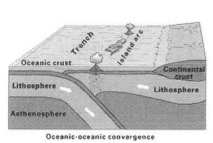 

(a) Subduction of an ocean plate beneath an ocean plate results in a volcanic island arc, an ocean trench and many earthquakes. (b) Japan is an arc-shaped island arc composed of volcanoes off the Asian mainland, as seen in this satellite image.

An animation of an ocean continent plate boundary is seen here:
http://www.iris.edu/hq/files/programs/education_and_outreach/aotm/11/AOTM_09_01_Convergent_480.mov.

Continent-continent: Continental plates are too buoyant to subduct. What happens to continental material when it collides? Since it has nowhere to go but up, this creates some of the world's largest mountains ranges (Figure opposite). Magma cannot penetrate this thick crust so there are no volcanoes, although the magma stays in the crust. Metamorphic rocks are common because of the stress the continental crust experiences. With enormous slabs of crust smashing together, continent-continent collisions bring on numerous and large earthquakes.

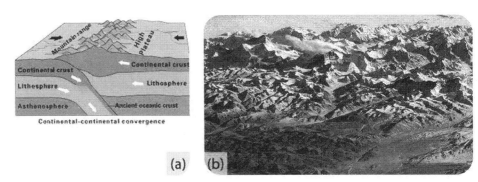

(a) (b)

(a) In continent-continent convergence, the plates push upward to create a high mountain range. (b) The world's highest mountains, the Himalayas, are the result of the collision of the Indian Plate with the Eurasian Plate, seen in this photo from the International Space Station.

A short animation of the Indian Plate colliding with the Eurasian Plate:
http://www.scotese.com/indianim.htm.

An animation of the Himalaya rising:
http://www.youtube.com/watch?v=ep2_axAA9Mw&NR=1.

The Appalachian Mountains are the remnants of a large mountain range that was created when North America rammed into Eurasia about 250 million years ago.

Transform Plate Boundaries

Transform plate boundaries are seen as transform faults, where two plates move past each other in opposite directions. Transform faults on continents bring massive earthquakes (Figure below).

At the San Andreas Fault in California, the Pacific Plate is sliding northeast relative to the North American plate, which is moving southwest. At the northern end of the picture, the transform boundary turns into a subduction zone.

California is very geologically active. What are the three major plate boundaries in or near California (Figure below)?

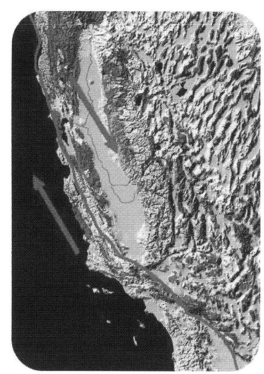

- **A transform plate boundary between the Pacific and North American plates creates the San Andreas Fault, the world's most notorious transform fault.**
- **Just offshore, a divergent plate boundary, Juan de Fuca ridge, creates the Juan de Fuca plate.**
- **A convergent plate boundary between the Juan de Fuca oceanic plate and the North American continental plate creates the Cascades volcanoes.**

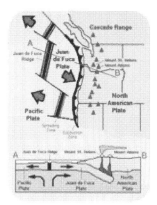

This map shows the three major plate boundaries in or near California.

A brief review of the three types of plate boundaries and the structures that are found there is the subject of this wordless video: http://www.youtube.com/watch?v=ifke1GsjNNO (4:50).

CHAPTER 3

ATMOSPHERE

STANDARD 3: STUDENTS WILL UNDERSTAND THE ATMOSPHERIC PROCESSES THAT SUPPORT LIFE AND CAUSE WEATHER AND CLIMATE.

Standard 3, Objective 1: Relate how energy from the Sun drives atmospheric processes and how atmospheric currents transport matter and transfer energy.

Objective 1
- Compare and contrast the amount of energy coming from the Sun that is reflected, absorbed or scattered by the atmosphere, oceans, and land masses.
- Construct a model that demonstrates how the greenhouse effect contributes to atmospheric energy.
- Conduct an investigation on how the tilt of Earth's axis causes variations in the intensity and duration of sunlight striking Earth.
- Explain how uneven heating of Earth's atmosphere at the equator and polar regions combined with the Coriolis effect create an atmospheric circulation system including, Hadley cells, trade winds, and prevailing westerlies, that moves heat energy around Earth.
- Explain how the presence of ozone in the stratosphere is beneficial to life, while ozone in the troposphere is considered an air pollutant.

EARTH'S ATMOSPHERE

Introduction
Why is Earth the only planet in the solar system known to have life? The main reason is Earth's atmosphere. The atmosphere is a mixture of gases that surrounds the planet. We also call it air. The gases in the air include nitrogen, oxygen, and carbon dioxide. Along with water vapor, air allows life to survive. Without it, Earth would be a harsh, barren world.

The Atmosphere and the Sun's Rays

The atmosphere protects living things from the sun's most harmful rays. Gases reflect or absorb the strongest rays of sunlight.

The atmosphere shields Earth from harmful solar rays.

104

The Atmosphere and Earth's Temperature

Gases in the atmosphere surround Earth like a blanket. They keep the temperature in a range that can support life. The gases keep out some of the sun's scorching heat during the day. At night, they hold the heat close to the surface, so it doesn't radiate out into space.

How does the atmosphere resemble a greenhouse?

To extend the growing season, many farmers use greenhouses. A greenhouse traps heat so that days that might be too cool for a growing plant can be made to be just right. Similar to a greenhouse, the atmosphere of the Earth traps the energy of the sun to keep our planet warm. This makes life on Earth possible.

The Greenhouse Effect

The role of greenhouse gases in the atmosphere is very important to balancing Earth's temperature. Greenhouse gases warm the atmosphere by absorbing and re-emitting heat. Some of the heat that radiates out from the ground is absorbed and re-emitted by greenhouse gases in the troposphere. Like a blanket on a sleeping person, greenhouse gases act as insulation for the planet. The warming of the atmosphere because of insulation by greenhouse gases is called the greenhouse effect (see Figure below). Greenhouse gases are the component of the atmosphere that moderate Earth's temperatures.

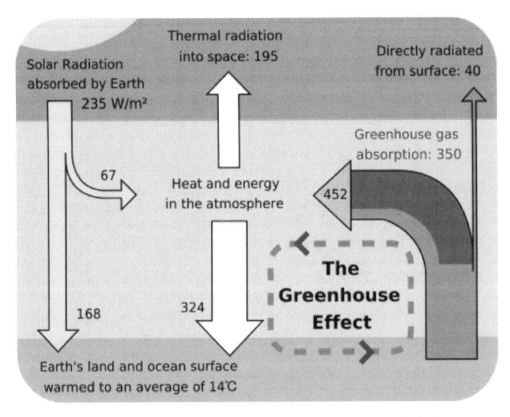

The Earth's heat budget shows the amount of energy coming into and going out of the Earth's system and the importance of the greenhouse effect. The numbers indicate a measurement of energy and the arrows depict the direction of the movement of the energy.

Greenhouse Gases

Greenhouse gases include carbon dioxide (CO_2), water vapor (H_2O), methane (CH_4), ozone (O_3), nitrous oxides (NO and NO_2), and chlorofluorocarbons (CFCs). All are a normal part of the atmosphere except CFCs. The Table below shows how each greenhouse gas naturally enters the atmosphere.

Greenhouse Gas Entering the Atmosphere	
Greenhouse Gas	Where It Comes From
Carbon dioxide	Respiration, volcanic eruptions, decomposition of plant material; burning of fossil fuels
Methane	Decomposition of plant material under some conditions, biochemical reactions in stomachs
Nitrous oxide	Produced by bacteria
Ozone	Atmospheric processes
Chlorofluorocarbons	Not naturally occurring; made by humans

Different greenhouse gases have different abilities to trap heat. For example, one methane molecule traps 23 times as much heat as one CO_2 molecule. One CFC-12 molecule (a type of CFC) traps 10,600 times as much heat as one CO_2. Still, CO_2 is a very important greenhouse gas because it is much more abundant in the atmosphere and has increased by over 40% since the industrial revolution.

HUMAN ACTIVITY AND GREENHOUSE GAS LEVELS

Human activity has significantly raised the levels of many of greenhouse gases in the atmosphere. Methane levels are about 2 1/2 times higher as a result of human activity. Carbon dioxide has increased more than 35%. CFCs have only recently existed. What do you think happens as atmospheric greenhouse gas levels increase? More greenhouse gases trap more heat and warm the atmosphere. The increase or decrease of greenhouse gases in the atmosphere affect climate and weather the world over.

For additional help check out this PowerPoint review, Atmospheric Energy and Global Temperatures, it looks at the movement of energy through the atmosphere http://www.youtube.com/watch?v=p6xMF_FFUUO (8:17).

SUMMARY

- Greenhouse gases include CO2, H2O, methane, O3, nitrous oxides (NO and NO2), and chlorofluorocarbons (CFCs).
- Tropospheric greenhouse gases trap heat in the atmosphere; greenhouse gases vary in their heat-trapping abilities.
- Levels of greenhouse gases in the atmosphere are increasing due to human activities.

Practice

Use this resource to answer the questions that follow.

http://www.hippocampus.org/Earth Science ⟶ Environmental Science ⟶ Search: Greenhouse Effects (first resource, starts with "About 50% of solar radiation...")

1. How much solar radiation is absorbed by the surface of the Earth?
2. What reflects the radiation?
3. How is most radiation re-emitted?
4. What is the net effect of this heating?
5. What are the primary greenhouse gases?

Review

1. If you were trying to keep down global temperature and you had a choice between adding 100 methane molecules or 1 CFC-12 molecule to the atmosphere, which would you choose? Why?
2. What is the greenhouse effect?
3. How does Earth's atmosphere resemble a greenhouse?

ENERGY AND LATITUDE

This is Antarctica. What season is this? Which is night and which is day?

The sun is always up, even in the middle of the night in Antarctica during the summer. The photo on the left is Antarctica during the night in the summer. The photo on the right is Antarctica during the day in summer. Similarly, in the winter Antarctica is mostly dark all day.

Different parts of Earth's surface receive different amounts of sunlight. You can see this in the Figure below. The sun's rays strike Earth's surface most directly at the equator. This focuses the rays on a small area. Near the poles, the sun's rays strike the surface at a slant. This spreads the rays over a wide area. The more focused the rays are, the more energy an area receives and the warmer it is. Another way to word this is that towards the poles there is a greater amount of area that receives that same amount of sunlight.

The lowest latitudes get the most energy from the sun. The highest latitudes get the least.

The Sun's Rays and Latitude

Sun's rays spread over a wide area.

Sun's rays spread over a narow area.

Sun's rays spread over a wide area.

The difference in solar energy received at different latitudes drives atmospheric circulation. Places that get more solar energy have more heat. Places that get less solar energy have less heat. Warm air rises and cool air sinks. These principles mean that air moves around the planet. The heat moves around the globe in certain ways. This determines the way the atmosphere moves.

SUMMARY

- A lot of the solar energy that reaches Earth hits the equator.
- Much less solar energy gets to the poles.
- The difference in the amount of solar energy drives atmospheric circulation.

Practice

Use this resource to answer the questions that follow.

http://www.kidsgeo.com/geography-for-kids/0074-latitude-effects-temperature.php

1. What is latitude?
2. What does latitude means to the heating of the Earth?
3. Why do high latitudes receive less sunlight?
4. What is the angle of incidence?

Review

5. The North Pole receives sunlight 24 hours a day in the summer. Why does it receive less solar radiation than the equator?
6. What part of Earth receives the most solar radiation in a year?
7. What makes the atmosphere move the way it does?

EARTH'S ENERGY BUDGET

How does heat on Earth resemble a household budget?

After the sun's energy enters the Earth's atmosphere the heat is either absorbed, reflected, or scattered. The amount left on Earth is equal to the amount of heat absorbed minus the amount of heat given off. If more energy comes into the system than goes out of the system, the planet warms. If less energy goes into the system than goes out of the system, the planet cools. Replace the word "money" for "heat" and "on Earth" to "in your bank account" and you describe a household budget. Of course, Earth's heat budget is a lot more complex than a simple household budget.

Heat at Earth's Surface

About half of the solar radiation that strikes the top of the atmosphere is filtered out before it reaches the ground. This energy can be absorbed by atmospheric gases, reflected by clouds, or scattered. Scattering occurs when a light wave strikes a particle and bounces off in some other direction.

About 3% of the energy that strikes the ground is reflected back into the atmosphere. The rest is absorbed by rocks, soil, and water and then radiated back into the air as heat. These infrared wavelengths of energy can only be seen by infrared sensors.

The basics of Earth's annual heat budget are described in this video:
http://www.youtube.com/watch?v=mjj2i3hNQFO&feature=related (5:40)

The Heat Budget

Because solar energy continually enters Earth's atmosphere and ground surface, is the planet getting hotter? The answer is no (although the next section contains an exception), because energy from Earth escapes into space through the top of the atmosphere. If the amount that exits is equal to the amount that comes in, then average global temperature stays the same. This means that the planet's heat budget is in balance. What happens if more energy comes in than goes out? If more energy goes out than comes in? To say that the Earth's heat budget is balanced ignores an important point. The amount of incoming solar energy is different at different latitudes. Where do you think the most solar energy ends up and why? Where does the least solar energy end up and why? See the Table below

The Amount of Incoming Solar Energy				
	Day Length	Sun Angle	Solar Radiation	Albedo
Equatorial Region	Nearly the same all year	High	High	Low
Polar Regions	Night 6 months	Low	Low	High

Note: Colder temperatures mean more ice and snow cover the ground, making albedo relatively high.

This animation shows the average surface temperature across the planet as it changes through the year:
Monthly Mean Temperatures http://upload.wikimedia.org/wikipedia/commons/b/b3/MonthlyMeanT.gif

SUMMARY

- The difference in solar energy received at different latitudes drives atmospheric circulation.
- Incoming solar radiation is absorbed by atmospheric gases, reflected by clouds, or scattered.
- Much of the radiation that strikes the ground is radiated back into the atmosphere as heat.
- More solar radiation strikes the equator than the poles.

Practice
Use this resource to answer the questions that follow:
http://www.youtube.com/watch?v=JFfD6jn_OvA

1. What does CERES measure?
2. What does the acronym CERES stand for?
3. What is the ideal radiation budget?
4. How much of the sun's radiation is reflected?
5. How much energy does the ocean absorb?
6. What are scientists finding with CERES?
7. Why is the Earth warming?
8. What is a carbon footprint?

Review
9. If the Sun suddenly started to emit more energy, what would happen to Earth's heat budget and the planet's temperature?
10. If more greenhouse gases were added to the atmosphere, what would happen to Earth's heat budget and the planet's temperature?
11. 3. What happens to sunlight that strikes the ground?

ATMOSPHERIC CIRCULATION

Why do we say Earth's temperature is moderate?
It may not look like it, but various processes work to moderate Earth's temperature across the latitudes. Atmospheric circulation brings warm equatorial air toward the poles and frigid polar air toward the equator. If the planet had an atmosphere that was stagnant (not moving), the difference in temperature between the two regions would be much greater.

The atmosphere is divided into various layers (as seen right). Weather happens in the lowest layer or the Troposphere.

Layers of the Atmosphere

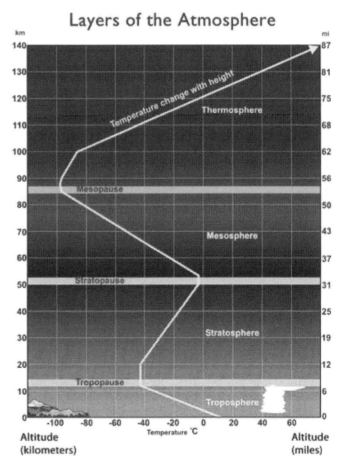

Air Pressure Zones

Within the troposphere are convection cells (see Figure right). Air heated at the ground rises, creating a low pressure zone. Air from the surrounding area is sucked into the space left by the rising air. Air flows horizontally at top of the troposphere; horizontal flow is called advection. The air cools until it descends. When the air reaches the ground, it creates a high pressure zone. Air flowing from areas of high pressure to low pressure creates winds. The greater the pressure difference between the pressure zones, the faster the wind blows.

Warm air rises, creating a low pressure zone; cool air sinks, creating a high pressure zone.

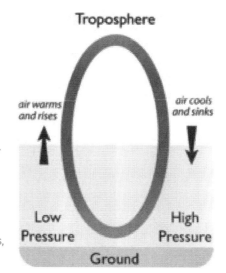

Warm air can hold more moisture than cool air. When warm air rises and cools in a low pressure zone, it may not be able to hold all the water it contains as vapor. Some water vapor may condense to form clouds or precipitation. When cool air descends, it warms. Since it can then hold more moisture, the descending air will evaporate water on the ground.

Wind

Air moving between large high and low pressure systems at the bases of the three major convection cells creates the global wind belts. These planet-wide air circulation systems profoundly affect regional climate. Smaller pressure systems create localized winds that affect the weather and climate of a local area.

An online guide to air pressure and winds from the University of Illinois is found here:
http://ww2010.atmos.uiuc.edu/%28Gh%29/guides/mtr/fw/home.rxml

Two Convection Cells

Because more solar energy hits the equator, the air warms and forms a low pressure zone. At the top of the troposphere, half moves toward the North Pole and half toward the South Pole. As it moves along the top of the troposphere it cools. The cool air is dense, and when it reaches a high pressure zone it sinks to the ground. The air is sucked back toward the low pressure at the equator. This describes the convection cells north and south of the equator.

Coriolis Effect

If the Earth did not rotate, there would be one convection cell in the northern hemisphere and one in the southern with the rising air at the equator and the sinking air at each pole. But because the planet does rotate, the situation is more complicated. The planet's rotation means that the Coriolis effect must be taken into account.

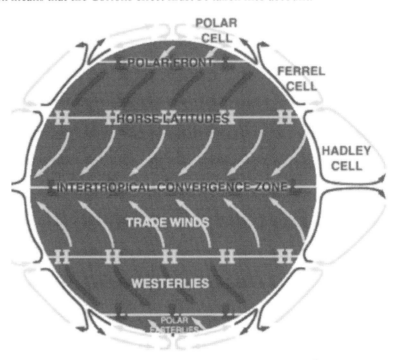

The atmospheric circulation cells, showing direction of winds at Earth's surface.

Let's look at atmospheric circulation in the Northern Hemisphere as a result of the Coriolis effect (see Figure above). Air rises at the equator, but as it moves toward the pole at the top of the troposphere, it deflects to the right. (Remember that it just appears to deflect to the right because the ground beneath it moves.) At about 30oN latitude, the air from the equator meets air flowing toward the equator from the higher latitudes. This air is cool because it has come from higher latitudes. Both batches of air descend, creating a high pressure zone. Once on the ground, the air returns to the equator. This convection cell is called the Hadley Cell and is found between 0o and 30oN.

Northern Hemisphere Convection Cells

There are two more convection cells in the Northern Hemisphere. The Ferrell cell is between 30oN and 50o to 60oN. This cell shares its southern, descending side with the Hadley cell to its south. Its northern rising limb is shared with the Polar cell located between 50oN to 60oN and the North Pole, where cold air descends.

Southern Hemisphere Convection Cells

There are three mirror image circulation cells in the Southern Hemisphere. In that hemisphere, the Coriolis effect makes objects appear to deflect to the left. The total number of atmospheric circulation cells around the globe is six.

SUMMARY

- The atmosphere has six major convection cells, three in the northern hemisphere and three in the southern.
- Coriolis effect results in there being three convection cells per hemisphere rather than one.
- Winds blow at the base of the atmospheric convection cells.

Practice

Use this resource to answer the questions that follow.

http://www.youtube.com/watch?v=DHrapzHPCSA

1. Where is insolation strongest?
2. What type of pressure occurs at the equator?
3. What type of pressure occurs at the poles?
4. What are Hadley cells?
5. Where does convection occur?
6. How do surface winds move?
7. What is the polar front?
8. How does air move at high altitudes?

Review

9. Diagram and label the parts of a convection cell in the troposphere.
10. How many major atmospheric convection cells would there be without Coriolis effect? Where would they be?
11. How does Coriolis effect change atmospheric convection?

GLOBAL WIND SYSTEMS

Why were winds so important to the early explorers?

When Columbus sailed the ocean blue, and for centuries before and after, ocean travel depended on the wind. Mariners knew how to get where they were going and at what time of the year based on experience with the winds. Winds were named for their usefulness to sailors, such as the trade winds that enabled commerce between people on opposite shores.

Global Wind Belts

Global winds blow in belts encircling the planet. Notice that the locations of these wind belts correlate (go along with) with the atmospheric circulation cells. Air blowing at the base of the circulation cells, from high pressure to low pressure, creates the global wind belts.

The global wind belts are enormous and the winds are relatively steady (see Figure below).

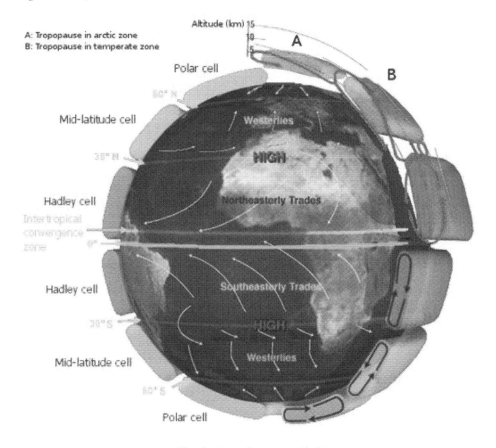

The direction of major wind belts.

The Global Winds

Let's look at the global wind belts in the Northern Hemisphere.

- In the Hadley cell air should move north to south, but it is deflected to the right by the Coriolis effect. So the air blows from northeast to the southwest. This belt is the trade winds, so called because at the time of sailing ships they were good for trade.
- In the Ferrel cell air should move south to north, but the winds actually blow from the southwest. This belt is also known as the westerly winds or westerlies.
- In the Polar cell, the winds travel from the northeast and are called the polar easterlies.

The wind belts are named for the directions from which the winds come. The westerly winds, for example, blow from west to east. These names hold for the winds in the wind belts of the Southern Hemisphere as well.

This video lecture discusses the 3-cell model of atmospheric circulation and the resulting global wind belts and surface wind currents:
http://www.youtube.com/watch?v=HWFDKdxK75E&feature=related (8:45).

Global Winds And Precipitation

The high and low pressure areas created by the six atmospheric circulation cells also determine in a general way the amount of precipitation a region receives. Rain is common in low pressure regions due to rising air. Air sinking in high pressure areas causes evaporation; these regions are usually dry. These features have a great deal of influence on climate.

Polar Front

The polar front is the junction between the Ferrell and Polar cells. At this low pressure zone, relatively warm, moist air of the Ferrell Cell runs into relatively cold, dry air of the Polar cell. The weather where these two meet is extremely variable, typical of much of North America and Europe.

Jet Stream

The polar jet stream is found high up in the atmosphere where the Polar Cell and Ferrel Cells come together. A jet stream is a fast-flowing river of air at the boundary between the troposphere and the stratosphere. Jet streams form where there is a large temperature difference between two air masses. This explains why the polar jet stream is the world's most powerful (Figure below).

A cross section of the atmosphere with major circulation cells and jet streams. The polar jet stream is the site of extremely turbulent weather.

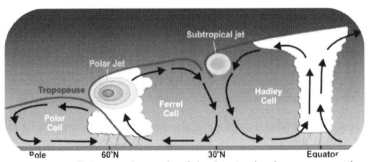

Jet streams move seasonally just as the angle of the Sun in the sky moves north and south. The polar jet stream, known as "the jet stream," moves south in the winter and north in the summer between about 30oN and 50o to 75oN.

SUMMARY

- Global winds blow from high to low pressure at the base of the atmospheric circulation   cells.
- The winds at the bases of the cells have names: the Hadley cell is the trade winds, the   Ferrel Cell is the westerlies, and the polar cell is the polar easterlies.
- Where two cells meet, weather can be extreme, particularly at the polar front.

Practice

Use this resource to answer the questions that follow.

http://www.youtube.com/watch?v=IWjeHtdpFjE

1. What creates wind?
2. What are monsoons? How are they created?
3. What are local and regional winds?
4. What are the global wind patterns?
5. In what direction does the Earth rotate?
6. What is the Coriolis effect?
7. What are the Westerlies?

Review

8. What is a jet stream? What is "the" jet stream?
9. Why does a flight across the United States from San Francisco to New York City takes less time than the reverse trip?
10. Where on a circulation cell is there typically precipitation and where is there typically evaporation?

OZONE AND THE ATMOSPHERE

Why can't the children in Punta Arenas go outside in the spring?

Children in Punta Arenas, Chile, the world's most southern city, look forward to spring as much as anyone who lives through a frigid, dark winter. But some years, the children are instructed not to go outside because the ozone hole has moved north and the UV radiation is too high.

Ozone Makes Life on Earth Possible

Ozone is a molecule composed of three oxygen atoms, (O_3). Ozone in the upper atmosphere absorbs high-energy ultraviolet (UV) radiation coming from the Sun. This protects living things on Earth's surface from the Sun's most harmful rays. Without ozone for protection, only the simplest life forms would be able to live on Earth. The highest concentration of ozone is in the ozone layer in the lower stratosphere.

Keeps Earth's Temperature Moderate

Along with the oceans, the atmosphere keeps Earth's temperatures within an acceptable range. Without an atmosphere, Earth's temperatures would be frigid at night and scorching during the day. If the 12-year-old in the scenario above asked why, she would find out. Greenhouse gases trap heat in the atmosphere. Important greenhouse gases include carbon dioxide, methane, water vapor, and ozone.

Ozone Depletion

At this point you might be asking yourself, "Is ozone bad or is ozone good?" There is no simple answer to that question: It depends on where the ozone is located (see Figure below).

- **In the troposphere, ozone is a pollutant.**
- **In the ozone layer in the stratosphere, ozone screens out high energy ultraviolet radiation and makes Earth habitable.**

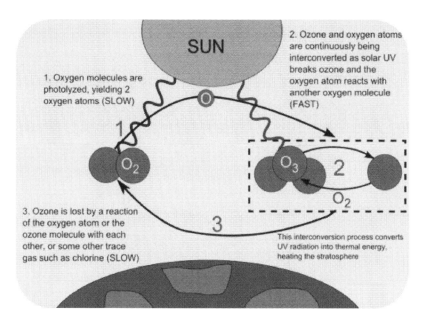

Solar energy breaks apart oxygen molecules into two oxygen atoms. (2) Ozone forms when oxygen atoms bond together as O3. UV rays break apart the ozone molecules into one oxygen molecule (O2) and one oxygen atom (O). These processes convert UV radiation into heat, which is how the Sun heats the stratosphere. (3) Under natural circumstances, the amount of ozone created equals the amount destroyed. When O3 interacts with chlorine or some other gases the O3 breaks down into O2 and O and so the ozone layer loses its ability to filter out UV.

How Ozone Is Destroyed

Human-made chemicals are breaking ozone molecules in the ozone layer. Chlorofluorocarbons (CFCs) are the most common, but there are others, including halons, methyl bromide, carbon tetrachloride, and methyl chloroform. CFCs were once widely used because they are cheap, nontoxic, nonflammable, and non-reactive. They were used as spray-can propellants, refrigerants, and in many other products.

Once they are released into the air, CFCs float up to the stratosphere. Air currents move them toward the poles. In the winter, they freeze onto nitric acid molecules in polar stratospheric clouds (PSC) (see Figure below). In the spring, the sun's warmth starts the air moving, and ultraviolet light breaks the CFCs apart. The chlorine atom floats away and attaches to one of the oxygen atoms on an ozone molecule. The chlorine pulls the oxygen atom away, leaving behind an O2 molecule, which provides no UV protection. The chlorine then releases the oxygen atom and moves on to destroy another ozone molecule. One CFC molecule can destroy as many as 100,000 ozone molecules.

PSCs form only where the stratosphere is coldest, and are most common above Antarctica in the wintertime. PSCs are needed for stratospheric ozone to be destroyed.

The Ozone Hole

Ozone destruction creates the ozone hole where the layer is dangerously thin (see Figure below). As air circulates over Antarctica in the spring, the ozone hole expands northward over the southern continents, including Australia, New Zealand, southern South America, and southern Africa. UV levels may rise as much as 20% beneath the ozone hole. The hole was first measured in 1981 when it was 2 million square km (900,000 square miles). The 2006 hole was the largest ever observed at 28 million square km (11.4 million square miles). The size of the ozone hole each year depends on many factors, including whether conditions are right for the formation of PSCs.

The September 2006 ozone hole, the largest observed (through 2011). Blue and purple colors show particularly low levels of ozone.

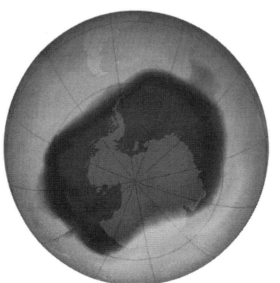

Find out how the ozone hole forms and view the hole over time on this National Geographic video:
http://news.nationalgeographic.com/news/2008/11/081103-ozone-video-vin.html.

Ozone Loss In The North

Ozone loss also occurs over the North Polar Region, but it is not enough for scientists to call it a hole. Why do you think there is less ozone loss over the North Pole area? The region of low ozone levels is small because the atmosphere is not as cold and PSCs do not form as readily. Still, springtime ozone levels are relatively low. This low moves south over some of the world's most populated areas in Europe, North America, and Asia. At 40oN, the latitude of New York City, UV-B has increased about 4% per decade since 1978. At 55oN, the approximate latitude of Moscow and Copenhagen, the increase has been 6.8% per decade since 1978.

This video explains an importance of the stratospheric ozone layer to life on Earth:
http://www.youtube.com/watch?v=I1wrEvc2URE&feature=related(1:52).

This NASA video discusses the ingredients of ozone depletion of Antarctica and the future of the ozone hole, including the effect of climate change:
http://www.youtube.com/watch?v=qUfVMogldr8&feature=related (2:20).

Effects Of Ozone Loss

Ozone losses on human health and environment include:

- Increases in sunburns, cataracts (clouding of the lens of the eye), and skin cancers. A loss   of ozone of only 1% is estimated to increase skin cancer cases by 5% to 6%.
- Decreases in the human immune system's ability to fight off infectious diseases.
- Reduction in crop yields because many plants are sensitive to ultraviolet light.
- Decreases in phytoplankton productivity. A decrease of 6% to 12% has been measured around Antarctica, which may be at least partly related to the ozone hole. The effects of excess UV on other organisms is not known.
- Whales in the Gulf of California have been found to have sunburned cells in their lowest skin layers, indicating very severe sunburns. The problem is greatest with light colored species or species that spend more time near the sea surface.

When the problem with ozone depletion was recognized, world leaders took action. CFCs were banned in spray cans in some nations in 1978. The greatest production of CFCs was in 1986, but it has declined since then. This will be discussed more in the next lesson.

SUMMARY

- CFCs float up into the stratosphere where they break apart. The chlorine pulls an oxygen ion off of an ozone molecule and destroys it.
- The ozone hole is where there is less ozone than normal at that altitude. It forms in the spring.
- Ozone loss increases the amount of high-energy ultraviolet radiation that can strike Earth, causing ecological and health problems.

Practice

Use these resources to answer the questions that follow.

http://www.youtube.com/watch?v=xD0FJ5xoGmw

1. What is the purpose of the ozone?
2. Why is the ozone layer so fragile?
3. How much did ozone decrease between 1979 and 1993?
4. Which satellite was launched to study the ozone? When?

http://www.youtube.com/watch?v=NvtUYQ_eAwY

5. What caused this ozone loss?

Review

6. How do CFCs destroy ozone?
7. What is the ozone hole and where is it found? Is there an equivalent hole in the Northern Hemisphere?
8. What are some of the consequences of ozone loss that have been identified?

STANDARD 3, OBJECTIVE 2: DESCRIBE ELEMENTS OF WEATHER AND THE FACTORS THAT CAUSE THEM TO VARY FROM DAY TO DAY.

Learning Objectives

- Identify the elements of weather and the instruments used to measure them (e.g., temperature—thermometer; precipitation—rain gauge or Doppler radar; humidity— hygrometer; air pressure—barometer; wind—anemometer; cloud coverage—satellite imaging).
- Describe conditions that give rise to severe weather phenomena (e.g., thunderstorms, tornados, hurricanes, El Niño/La Niña).
- Explain a difference between a low pressure system and a high pressure system, including the weather associated with them.
- Diagram and describe cold, warm, occluded, and stationary boundaries (weather fronts) between air masses.
- Design and conduct a weather investigation, use an appropriate display of the data, and interpret the observations and data.

Now that we have looked at the atmosphere lets bring it a little closer to home and talk about weather. For an overview of air masses, see:
http://www.teachengineering.org/view_lesson.php?url=collection/cub_/lessons/cub_weather/cub_weather_lesson02.xml

AIR MASSES

An air mass is a large body of air that has about the same conditions throughout. For example, an air mass might have cold dry air. Another air mass might have warm moist air. The conditions in an air mass depend on where the air mass formed.

Formation of Air Masses

Most air masses form over polar or tropical regions. They may form over continents or oceans. Air masses are moist if they form over oceans. They are dry if they form over continents. Air masses that form over oceans are called maritime air masses. Those that form over continents are called continental air masses. Figure 7.3 shows air masses that form over or near North America.

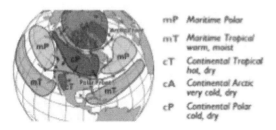

mP   Maritime Polar

mT   Maritime Tropical
     warm, moist

cT   Continental Tropical
     hot, dry

cA   Continental Arctic
     very cold, dry

cP   Continental Polar
     cold, dry

North American air masses.

An air mass takes on the conditions of the area where it forms. For example, a continental polar air mass has cold dry air. A maritime polar air mass has cold moist air. Which air masses have warm moist air? Where do they form?

Movement of Air Masses

When a new air mass goes over a region it brings its characteristics to the region. This may change the area's temperature and humidity. Moving air masses cause the weather to change when they contact different conditions. For example, a warm air mass moving over cold ground may cause an inversion.

Why do air masses move? Winds and jet streams push them along. Cold air masses tend to move toward the equator. Warm air masses tend to move toward the poles. Coriolis effect causes them to move on a diagonal. Many air masses move toward the northeast over the U.S. This is the same direction that global winds blow.

FRONTS

When cold air masses move south from the poles, they run into warm air masses moving north from the tropics. The boundary between two air masses is called a front. Air masses usually don't mix at a front. The differences in temperature and pressure cause clouds and precipitation. Types of fronts include cold, warm, occluded, and stationary fronts.

Cold Fronts

A cold front occurs when a cold air mass runs into a warm air mass. This is shown in Figure above. The cold air mass moves faster than the warm air mass and lifts the warm air mass out of its way. As the warm air rises, its water vapor condenses. Clouds form, and precipitation falls. If the warm air is very humid, precipitation can be heavy. Temperature and pressure differences between the two air masses cause winds. Winds may be very strong along a cold front.

As the fast-moving cold air mass keeps advancing, so does the cold front. Cold fronts often bring sudden changes in the weather. There may be a thin line of storms right at the front that moves as it moves. In the spring and summer, these storms may be thunderstorms and tornadoes. In the late fall and winter, snow storms may occur. After a cold front passes, the cold air mass behind it brings cooler temperatures. The air is likely to be less humid as well.

Warm Fronts

When a warm air mass runs into a cold air mass it creates a warm front. The warm air mass is moving faster than the cold air mass, so it flows up over the cold air mass. As the warm air rises, it cools, resulting in clouds and sometimes light precipitation. Warm fronts move slowly and cover a wide area. After a warm front passes, the warm air mass behind it brings warmer temperatures. The warm air is also likely to be more humid.

Occluded Fronts

With an occluded front, a warm air mass becomes trapped between two cold air masses. The warm air is lifted up above the cold air as in Figure 7.6. The weather at an occluded front is especially fierce right at the occlusion. Precipitation and shifting winds are typical.

Stationary Fronts

Sometimes two air masses stop moving when they meet. These stalled air masses create a stationary front. Such a front may bring clouds and precipitation to the same area for many days.

Cold Front

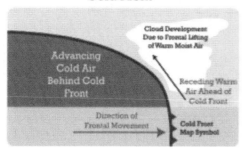

Cold fronts often bring stormy weather.

Warm Front

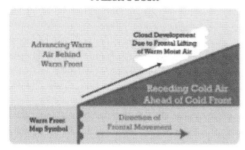

Warm fronts generally bring cloudy weather.

Occluded Front

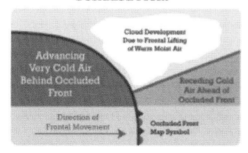

How does an occluded front differ from a warm or cold front?

LESSON SUMMARY

- An air mass is a large body of air that has about the same conditions throughout. Air masses take on the conditions of the area where they form. Winds and air currents cause air masses to move. Moving air masses cause changes in the weather.
- A front forms at the boundary between two air masses. Types of fronts include cold, warm, occluded, and stationary fronts. Clouds, precipitation, and storms commonly occur along fronts.
- A cyclone is a system of winds that rotates around a center of low air pressure. An anticyclone is a system of winds that rotates around a center of high air pressure.

LESSON REVIEW QUESTIONS

RECALL

1. What is an air mass?
2. Describe continental polar and maritime tropical air masses.
3. What causes air masses to move?
4. What is a front?
5. Define cyclone and anticyclone.

FORECASTING THE WEATHER

Weather instruments measure weather conditions. One of the most important conditions is air pressure, which is measured with a barometer. Figure right shows how a barometer works. There are also a number of other commonly used weather instruments:

- A thermometer measures temperature.
- An anemometer measures wind speed.
- A rain gauge measures the amount of rain.
- A hygrometer measures humidity.
- A wind vane shows wind direction.
- A snow gauge measures the amount of snow.

Barometer

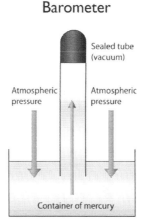

Sealed tube (vacuum)

Atmospheric pressure — Atmospheric pressure

Container of mercury

The greater the air pressure outside the tube, the higher the mercury rises inside the tube.

Weather Instruments

Thermometer (temperature)

Anemometer (wind speed)

Hygrometer (humidity)

Rain gauge (amount of rain)

Wind vane (wind direction)

Snow gauge (amount of snow)

Weather instruments collect data from all over the world at thousands of weather stations. Many are on land but some float in the oceans on buoys. There's probably at least one weather station near you. You can find out where at this link: http://lwf.ncdc.noaa.gov/oa/climate/stationlocator.htm

Other weather devices are needed to collect weather data in the atmosphere. They include weather balloons, satellites, and radar.

Weather stations contain many instruments for measuring weather conditions. The weather balloon will rise into the atmosphere until it bursts. As it rises, it will gather weather data and send it to the surface. Many weather satellites orbit Earth. They constantly collect and transmit weather data from high above the surface. A radar device sends out radio waves in all directions. The waves bounce off water in the atmosphere and then return to the sender. The radar data shows where precipitation is falling.

Using Computers

What do meteorologists do with all that weather data? They use it in weather models. The models analyze the data and predict the weather. The models require computers. That's because so many measurements and calculations are involved.

LESSON SUMMARY

- Weather is very complex. This makes it hard to predict. Certain "rules" can help. For example, low pressure brings stormy weather.
- Weather instruments measure weather factors. Weather stations collect data on Earth's surface. Weather balloons, satellites, and radar collect data in the atmosphere. Computer models analyze the data and help predict the weather.
- A weather map shows the weather for a certain area. It can show actual or predicted weather. It may show a single weather condition or more than one.

LESSON REVIEW QUESTIONS

RECALL
1. Why is weather difficult to predict?
2. List three weather instruments, and state what they measure.
3. What is the role of weather balloons and weather satellites?
4. What does a weather map show?

SEVERE WEATHER

Sometimes weather can change drastically. Have you ever been out on a nice sunny day and suddenly you see large billowing clouds overhead? There are several types of severe weather than can happen around the globe. What is happening in your neighborhood?

Thunderstorms

Thunderstorms form when ground temperatures are high, typically during late afternoons and early evenings in the summer.

Thunderstorms: Thunder and Lightning

- Thunder storms can form individually or as part of a squall line along a cold front.
- Large amounts of energy collected within cumulonimbus clouds is released as electricity called lightning
- The rapid heating of the air surrounding a lightning strike produces a loud clap of thunder, which is a result of the rapidly expanding air.

Tornadoes

Characteristics:

- Tornadoes form at the front of severe thunderstorms
- Tornadoes generally last only a few minutes
- When tornadoes form over water, they are referred to as waterspouts

Formation:

- Tornadoes are typically products of severe thunderstorms.
- As air in a thunderstorm rises, the surrounding air races in to fill the gap,
- This forms a funnel-shaped whirling column of air that extends down to the earth from the thundercloud.

Destruction:

- Damages a small area but can destroy everything it passes
- An average of 90 people are killed by tornadoes each year

Location:

- Tornadoes form during the spring where maritime tropical and continental polar air masses meet.

Hurricanes, typhoons, tornadoes, and cyclones... These terms can be confusing to differentiate from one another. A cyclone is the umbrella term that includes tropical storms and typhoons. Tornadoes and cyclones are considered different types of storms.

Hurricanes

Hurricanes are special types of cyclones that form in the tropics. They are also referred to as tropical cyclones.

Hurricanes: Formation

- Hurricanes arise in the tropical latitudes in summer and autumn when sea surface temperatures are over 28°C.
- Warm seas create a large humid air mass.
- Warm air rises and forms a low pressure cell called a tropical depression.
- Air begins to rotate around the low pressure.
- As air rises, water vapor condenses, releasing energy from latent heat.
- If wind shear is low, the storm will build into a hurricane within 2-3 days

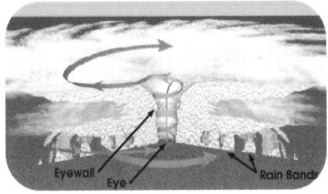

Blizzards

Blizzards are snowstorms large with high winds.

Conditions:

- Temperatures below −7° C (20° F); −12° C (10° F) for a severe blizzard.
- Winds greater than 56 kmh (35 mph); 72 kmh (45 mph) for a severe blizzard.
- Snow so heavy that visibility is 2/5 km (1/4 mile) or less for at least three hours; near zero visibility for a severe blizzard.

Blizzards: Formation

- Occur across the middle latitudes and towards the poles
- Usually part of a mid-latitude cyclone

- Commonly occurs when the jet stream has traveled south and a cold, northern air mass comes into contact with a warmer, semitropical air mass.
- Pressure gradient between the low-pressure and high-pressure parts of the storm create strong winds

Blizzards: Lake-Effect Snow

- Lake effect snow occurs when an air mass reaches the leeward side of a lake. The air mass is very unstable and drops a tremendous amount of snow.

Heat Waves and Droughts

Heat Wave:

- According to the World Meteorological Organization a region is in a heat wave if it has more than five consecutive days of temperatures that are more than 9° F (5° C) above average.
- A high-pressure area sitting over a region with no movement is the likely cause of a heat wave.

Drought:

- When a region gets significantly less precipitation than normal for an extended period of time, it is in drought.
- Consequences to droughts include dust storms, blown over soil, and wildlife disturbance.

SUMMARY

- A storm is an episode of severe weather. It is caused by a major disturbance in the atmosphere. Types of storms include thunderstorms, tornadoes, and hurricanes.
- A thunderstorm is a storm with heavy rains and lightning. It may also have hail and high winds. Thunderstorms are very common. They occur when the air is very warm and humid.
- A tornado is a storm with a funnel-shaped cloud. It has very strong, whirling winds. Tornadoes are small but powerful. They occur with thunderstorms and hurricanes.
- A hurricane is a large storm with high winds and heavy rains. Hurricanes develop from tropical cyclones. They form over warm ocean water. Much of the damage from hurricanes may be caused by storm surge.
- Winter storms develop from cyclones at higher latitudes. They include blizzards and lake-effect snow storms.

LESSON REVIEW QUESTIONS

RECALL
1. Define storm. List three types of storms.
2. Why do thunderstorms occur?
3. What is lightning? What causes it?
4. Where is tornado alley? Why do so many tornadoes occur there?
5. Where do hurricanes form? Where do they get their energy?

WHAT ARE SHORT-TERM CLIMATE CHANGES?

El Niño and La Niña bring about dramatic changes in climate for a year or two. In some locations one brings rain and the other brings drought. In California, for example, El Niño years are full of snow and rain. La Niña years tend towards drought. These variations can bring tremendous changes to living creatures. Humans are also affected; for example, erosion from storms may be very high some years.

Short-Term Climate Change

You've probably heard of El Niño and La Niña. These terms refer to certain short-term changes in climate. The changes are natural and occur in cycles, lasting from days to years. El Niño and La Niña are not the only short-term climate changes. Others include the Pacific decadal oscillation and the North Atlantic oscillation. El Niño and La Niña are the most noticeable and discussed.

To understand El Niño and La Niña, you first need to know what happens in normal years. This is shown in the Figure below.

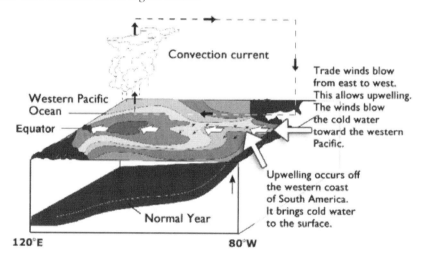

This diagram represents the Pacific Ocean in a normal year. North and South America are the found at the lower left and upper right of the image.

El Niño

During an El Niño, the western Pacific Ocean is warmer than usual. This causes the trade winds to change direction. The winds blow from west to east instead of east to west. This is shown in Figure below. The change in the trade winds also causes the jet streams to be north of their normal location. The warm water travels east across the equator, too.

Warm water piles up along the western coast of South America. This prevents upwelling. Why do you think this is true?

These changes in water temperature, winds, and currents affect climates worldwide. The changes usually last a year or two. Some places get more rain than normal. Other places get less. In many locations, the weather is more severe.

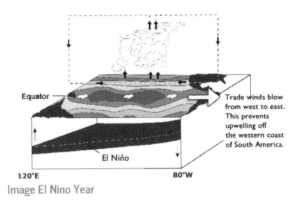

Image El Nino Year

How do you think El Niño affects climate on the western coast of South America? This ABC News video explores the relationship of El Niño to global warming. El Niño is named as the cause of strange weather across the United States in the winter of 2007 in this video:
http://www.youtube.com/watch?v=5uk9nwtAOio&feature=related (3:33).

La Niña

La Niña generally follows El Niño. It occurs when the Pacific Ocean is cooler than normal (see Figure below). The trade winds are like they are in a normal year. They blow from east to west. But in a La Niña the winds are stronger than usual. More cool water builds up in the western Pacific. These changes can also affect climates worldwide.

Image La Nina year

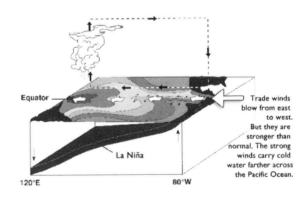

How do you think La Niña affects climate on the western coast of South America? Some scientists think that global warming is affecting the cycle of El Niño and La Niña. These short-term changes seem to be cycling faster now than in the past. They are also more extreme.

An online guide to El Niño and La Niña events from the University of Illinois is found here:http://ww2010.atmos.uiuc.edu/%28Gh%29/guides/mtr/eln/home.rxml. El Niño and La Niña are explained in a National Geographic vides found at National Geographic Video, Natural disaster, Landslides, and More: El Niño

CLIMATE

- Explain differences between weather and climate and the methods used to investigate evidence for changes in climate (e.g., ice core sampling, tree rings, historical temperature measurements, changes in the extent of alpine glaciers, changes in the extent of Arctic sea ice).

- Explain how Earth's climate has changed over time and describe the natural causes for these changes (e.g., Milankovitch cycles, solar fluctuations, plate tectonics).

  - Describe how human activity influences the carbon cycle and may contribute to climate change.

  - Explain the differences between air pollution and climate change and how these are related to society's use of fossil fuels.

Sometimes you hear about what the weather is like in an area. You also hear about what the climate is like in an area. What is the difference?

The Weather

- Weather describes what the atmosphere is like at a specific time and place.
- Weather is made up of factors including air temperature, pressure, fog, humidity, cloud cover, precipitation, and wind.
- Most of the time, the weather is different every day.

The Climate

- The climate of a region is the long-term average weather of a particular spot. It is often more predictable than the weather.
- The climate usually changes slowly, and is usually affected by factors like the angle of the Sun and the amount of cloud cover in the region.
- The weather changes all the time. It can change in a matter of minutes. Changes in climate occur more slowly. They also tend to be small changes. But even small changes in climate can make a big difference for Earth and its living things.

HOW EARTH'S CLIMATE HAS CHANGED

Earth's climate has changed many times. It's been both hotter and colder than it is today.

The Big Picture

Over much of Earth's past, the climate was probably a little warmer than it is today. But ice ages also occurred many times. An ice age is a period when temperatures are cooler than normal. This causes glaciers to spread to lower latitudes. Scientists think that ice ages occurred at least six times over the last billion years alone. How do scientists learn about Earth's past climates?

Pleistocene Ice Age

Pleistocene Glaciers

The last major ice age took place in the Pleistocene. This epoch lasted from 2 million to 14,000 years ago. Earth's temperature was only 5° C (9° F) cooler than it is today. But glaciers covered much of the Northern Hemisphere. In the Figure below, you can see how far south they went. Clearly, a small change in temperature can have a big impact on the planet. Humans lived during this ice age.

Pleistocene Glaciers. Chicago would have been buried under a glacier if it existed during the Pleistocene.

Earth's Recent Temperature

Since the Pleistocene, Earth's temperature has risen. Figure below shows how it changed over just the last 2000 years. There were minor ups and downs. But each time, the anomaly (the difference from average temperature) was less than 1° C (1.8° F).

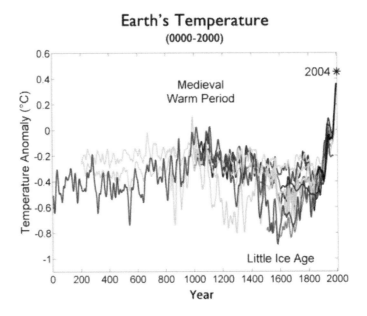

Earth

Since the mid 1800s, Earth has warmed up quickly. Look at the Figure below. The 14 hottest years on record occurred since 1900. Eight of them occurred since 1998. This is what is usually meant by global warming.

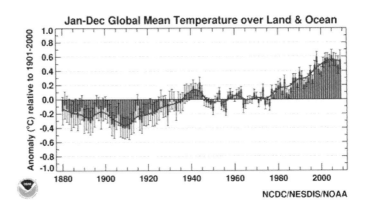

144

STANDARD 3, OBJECTIVE 3: EXAMINE THE NATURAL AND HUMAN-CAUSED PROCESSES THAT CAUSE EARTH'S CLIMATE TO CHANGE OVER INTERVALS OF TIME RANGING FROM DECADES TO MILLENNIA.

Natural processes caused early climate change. Human beings may be contributing to current climate change.

CAUSES OF CLIMATE CHANGE

- Several natural processes may affect Earth's temperature. They range from sunspots to Earth's wobble.
- Sunspots are storms on the sun. When the number of sunspots is high, the sun gives off more energy than usual. This may increase Earth's temperature.
- Plate movements cause continents to drift. They move closer to the poles or the equator. Ocean currents also shift when continents drift. All these changes affect Earth's temperature.
- Plate movements trigger volcanoes. A huge eruption could spew so much gas and ash into the air that little sunlight would reach the surface for months or years. This could lower Earth's temperature.
- A large asteroid hitting Earth would throw a lot of dust into the air. This could block sunlight and cool the planet.
- Earth goes through regular changes in its position relative to the sun. Its orbit changes slightly. Earth also wobbles on its axis. Both of these changes can affect Earth's temperature.

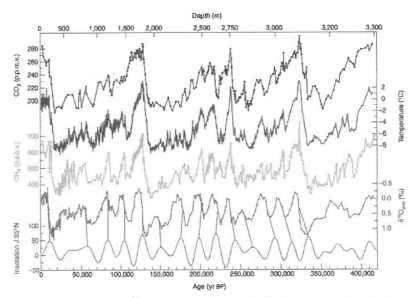

Image Vostok Ice Core. Why do the blue, green and red lines go in the same direction at the same time?

This is a complicated graph, but extremely interesting. The data are from the 3600 meter-long Vostok ice core, which gave climate scientists an unprecedented look into the history of Earth's climate. The red line is temperature. You can see that carbon dioxide and methane are correlated with temperature. When these greenhouse gases are high, temperature is high. This holds true for the 440,000 years revealed in the core.

Causes of Long-term Climate Change
Many processes can cause climate to change. These include changes:

- In the amount of energy the Sun produces over years.
- In the positions of the continents over millions of years.
- In the tilt of Earth's axis and orbit over thousands of years.
- That are sudden and dramatic because of random catastrophic events, such as a large asteroid impact.
- In greenhouse gases in the atmosphere, caused naturally or by human activities.

SOLAR VARIATION

The amount of energy the Sun radiates is variable. Sunspots are magnetic storms on the Sun's surface that increase and decrease over an 11-year cycle (Figure below). When the number of sunspots is high, solar radiation is also relatively high. But the entire variation in solar radiation is tiny relative to the total amount of solar radiation that there is, and there is no known 11-year cycle in climate variability. The Little Ice Age corresponded to a time when there were no sunspots on the Sun.

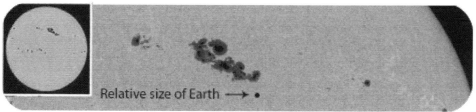

Relative size of Earth ⟶ •

Sunspots on the face of the Sun.

PLATE TECTONICS

Plate tectonic movements can alter climate. Over millions of years as seas open and close, ocean currents may distribute heat differently. For example, when all the continents are joined into one supercontinent (such as Pangaea), nearly all locations experience a continental climate. When the continents separate, heat is more evenly distributed. Plate tectonic movements may help start an ice age. When continents are located near the poles, ice can accumulate, which may increase albedo and lower global temperature. Low enough temperatures may start a global ice age.

Plate motions trigger volcanic eruptions, which release dust and CO_2 into the atmosphere. Ordinary eruptions, even large ones, have only a short-term effect on weather (Figure below). Massive eruptions of the fluid lavas that create lava plateaus release much more gas and dust, and can change climate for many years. This type of eruption is exceedingly rare; none has occurred since humans have lived on Earth.

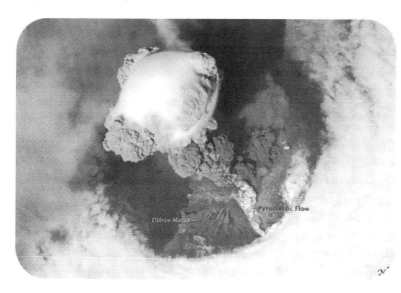

An eruption like Sarychev Volcano (Kuril Islands, northeast of Japan) in 2009 would have very little impact on weather.

MILANKOVITCH CYCLES

The most extreme climate of recent Earth history was the Pleistocene. Scientists attribute a series of ice ages to variation in the Earth's position relative to the Sun, known as Milankovitch cycles.

The Earth goes through regular variations in its position relative to the Sun:

1. The shape of the Earth's orbit changes slightly as it goes around the Sun. The orbit varies from more circular to more elliptical in a cycle lasting between 90,000 and 100,000 years. When the orbit is more elliptical, there is a greater difference in solar radiation between winter and summer.
2. The planet wobbles on its axis of rotation. At one extreme of this 27,000 year cycle, the Northern Hemisphere points toward the Sun when the Earth is closest to the Sun. Summers are much warmer and winters are much colder than now. At the opposite extreme, the Northern Hemisphere points toward the Sun when it is farthest from the Sun. This results in chilly summers and warmer winters.
3. The planet's tilt on its axis varies between 22.1o and 24.5o. Seasons are caused by the tilt of Earth's axis of rotation, which is at a 23.5o angle now. When the tilt angle is smaller, summers and winters differ less in temperature. This cycle lasts 41,000 years.

When these three variations are charted out, a climate pattern of about 100,000 years emerges. Ice ages correspond closely with Milankovitch cycles. Since glaciers can form only over land, ice ages only occur when landmasses cover the polar regions. Therefore, Milankovitch cycles are also connected to plate tectonics.

CHANGES IN ATMOSPHERIC GREENHOUSE GAS LEVELS

Since greenhouse gases trap the heat that radiates off the planet's surfaces, what would happen to global temperatures if atmospheric greenhouse gas levels decreased? What if greenhouse gases increased? A decrease in greenhouse gas levels decreases global temperature and an increase raises global temperature.

Greenhouse gas levels have varied throughout Earth history. For example, CO_2 has been present at concentrations less than 200 parts per million (ppm) and more than 5,000 ppm. But for at least 650,000 years, CO_2 has never risen above 300 ppm, during either glacial or interglacial periods (Figure below).

CO_2 levels during glacial (blue) and interglacial (yellow) periods. Are CO_2 levels relatively high or relatively low during interglacial periods? Current carbon dioxide levels are at 387 ppm, the highest level for the last 650,000 years. BP means years before present.

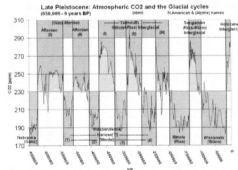

148

Natural processes add and remove CO2 from the atmosphere.

Processes that add CO2:
- **volcanic eruptions**
- **decay or burning of organic matter.**

Processes that remove CO2:
- **absorption by plant and animal tissue.**

When plants are turned into fossil fuels, the CO_2 in their tissue is stored with them. So CO_2 is removed from the atmosphere. What does this do to Earth's average temperature? What happens to atmospheric CO_2 when the fossil fuels are burned? What happens to global temperatures?

SUMMARY

- The positions of continents, the sizes of oceans and the amount of volcanic activity that takes place are all ways that plate tectonics processes can affect climate.
- Milankovitch cycles affect the way Earth relates to the sun due to the shape of the planet's orbit, its axial tilt, and its wobble.
- Atmospheric greenhouse gas levels correlate with average global temperatures.

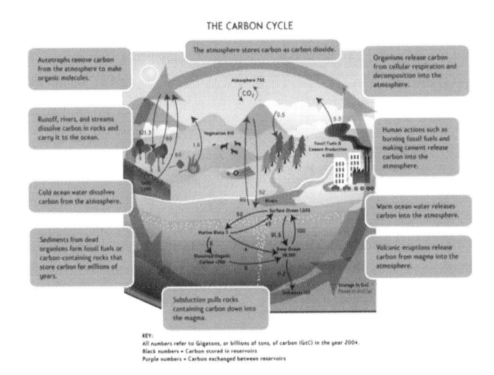

THE CARBON CYCLE

FORMATION OF FOSSIL FUELS

Fossil fuels are made from plants and animals that lived hundreds of millions of years ago. The plants used energy from the Sun to form energy-rich carbon compounds. As the plants and animals died, their remains settled onto the ground and at the bottom of the sea. Layer upon layer of organic material was laid down. Eventually, the layers were buried very deeply. They experienced intense heat and pressure. Over millions of years, the organic material turned into fossil fuels.

Fossil fuels are compounds of carbon and hydrogen, called hydrocarbons

Human Actions Impact the Carbon Cycle

Humans have changed the natural balance of the carbon cycle because we use coal, oil, and natural gas to supply our energy demands. Fossil fuels are a sink for CO_2 when they form, but they are a source for CO_2 when they are burned.

The equation for combustion of propane, which is a simple hydrocarbon looks like this (Figure below):

$$C_3H_8 + 5\,O_2 \rightarrow 3\,CO_2 + 4\,H_2O$$

$$\text{propane} \qquad \text{oxygen} \qquad \text{carbon dioxide} \qquad \text{water}$$

Propane combustion formula.

The equation shows that when propane burns, it uses oxygen and produces carbon dioxide and water. So when a car burns a tank of gas, the amount of CO_2 in the atmosphere increases just a little. Added over millions of tanks of gas and coal burned for electricity in power plants and all of the other sources of CO_2, the result is the increase in atmospheric CO_2 seen in the graph above.

The second largest source of atmospheric CO_2 is deforestation (Figure below). Trees naturally absorb CO_2 while they are alive. Trees that are cut down lose their ability to absorb CO_2. If the tree is burned or decomposes, it becomes a source of CO_2. A forest can go from being a carbon sink to being a carbon source.

This forest in Mexico has been cut down and burned to clear forested land for agriculture.

CAUSES OF GLOBAL WARMING

Recent global warming trends. Figure below shows the increase in carbon dioxide since 1960. Carbon dioxide is a greenhouse gas. It's one of several gasses in the air. This has created a greater greenhouse effect.

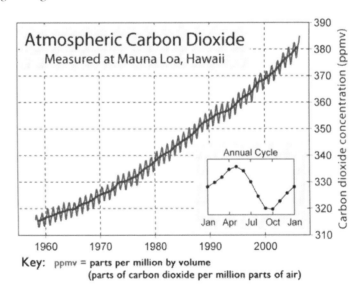

Key: ppmv = parts per million by volume
(parts of carbon dioxide per million parts of air)

How much more carbon dioxide was in the air in 2005 than in 1960?

EFFECTS OF GLOBAL WARMING

As Earth has gotten warmer, sea ice has melted. This has raised the level of water in the oceans. Figure below shows how much sea level has risen since 1880.

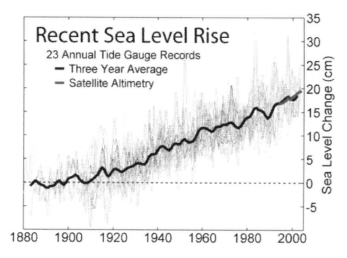

How much did sea level rise between 1880 and 2000?

Other effects of global warming may include more extreme weather. Many living things may not be able to adjust to the changing climate. For example, coral reefs are dying out in all the world's oceans due to climate change and other factors.

How Will Climate Change in the Future?

Look at the projections in Figure below. The temperature in 2100 may be as much as 5° C (9° F) higher than it was in 2000. A 5° C decrease in temperature led to the Pleistocene ice age. How might a 5° C increase in temperature affect Earth in the future?

Projections of several different models are shown here. They all predict a warmer future.

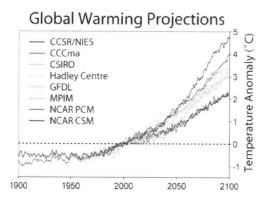

One effect of higher temperatures will be more melting of sea ice. The figure below shows how much less sea ice there may be in 2050 if temperatures keep going up. This would cause sea level to rise even higher. Some coastal cities could be under water. Millions of people would have to move inland. How might other living things be affected?

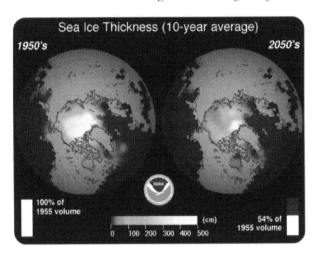

In the 2050s, there may be only half as much sea ice as there was in the 1950s.

Why is the atmosphere important?

Well, it contains all of the air that we breathe. The atmosphere also has other roles and functions, so when we interfere with the atmosphere, we interfere with some important biological processes. And this can have consequences.

The Atmosphere

The atmosphere plays an important part in maintaining Earth's freshwater supply. It is part of the water cycle. It refills lakes and rivers with precipitation. The atmosphere also provides organisms with gases needed for life. It contains oxygen for cellular respiration and carbon dioxide for photosynthesis.

AIR POLLUTION

Earth's atmosphere is vast. However, it has been seriously polluted by human activities. Air pollution consists of chemical substances and particles released into the atmosphere, mainly by human actions. The major cause of outdoor air pollution is the burning of fossil fuels. Power plants, motor vehicles, and home furnaces all burn fossil fuels and contribute to the problem (see Table below). Ranching and using chemicals such as fertilizers also cause air pollution. Erosion of soil in farm fields and construction sites adds dust particles to the air as well. Fumes from building materials, furniture, carpets, and paint add toxic chemicals to indoor air.

Pollutant	Example/Major Source	Problem
Sulfur oxides (SOx)	Coal-fired power plants	Acid Rain
Nitrogen oxides (NOx)	Motor vehicle exhaust	Acid Rain
Carbon monoxide (CO)	Motor vehicle exhaust	Poisoning
Carbon dioxide (CO2)	All fossil fuel burning	Global Warming
Particulate matter (smoke, dust)	Wood and coal burning	Respiratory disease, Global Dimming
Mercury	Coal-fired power plants, medical waste	Neurotoxicity
Smog	Coal burning	Respiratory problems; eye irritation
Ground-level ozone	Motor vehicle exhaust	Respiratory problems; eye irritation

In humans, air pollution causes respiratory and cardiovascular problems. In fact, more people die each year from air pollution than automobile accidents. Air pollution also affects ecosystems worldwide by causing acid rain, ozone depletion, and global warming. Ways to reduce air pollution from fossil fuels include switching to nonpolluting energy sources (such as solar energy) and using less energy. What are some ways you could use less energy?

Acid Rain

All life relies on a relatively narrow range of pH, or acidity. That's because protein structure and function are very sensitive to pH. Air pollution can cause precipitation to become acidic. Nitrogen and sulfur oxides, mainly from motor vehicle exhaust and coal burning, create acids when they combine with water in the air. The acids lower the pH of precipitation, forming acid rain. If acid rain falls on the ground, it may damage soil and soil organisms. If it falls on plants, it may kill them (see Figure below). If it falls into lakes, it lowers the pH of the water and kills aquatic organisms.

Image Effects of Acid Rain

Effects of Acid Rain. These trees in a European forest were killed by acid rain.

HYDROSPHERE

CHAPTER 4

Vocabulary

o   polarity

o   polar molecule

o   hydrogen bond

o   cohesion

o   adhesion

o   density

STANDARD 4: STUDENTS WILL UNDERSTAND THE DYNAMICS OF THE HYDROSPHERE.

Standard 4, Objective 1: Characterize the water cycle in terms of its reservoirs, water movement among reservoirs and how water has been recycled throughout time.

Lesson Objectives

- Describe the chemical makeup of water
- Understand the properties of water and why it can exist in all three states
- Describe the unique nature properties of water (cohesion, adhesion, surface tension, etc.) due to hydrogen bonding

Introduction

Dihydrogen oxide or dihydrogen monoxide. Does this chemical sound dangerous? Another name for this compound is...water. Water can create some absolutely beautiful sights. Iguassu Falls is the largest series of waterfalls on the planet, located in Brazil, Argentina, and Paraguay. Water is necessary for life. The importance of water to life cannot be emphasized enough. All life needs water. Life started in water. Essentially, without this simple three atom molecule, life would not exist.

Structure and Properties of Water

No doubt, you are already aware of some of the properties of water. For example, you probably know that water is tasteless and odorless. You also probably know that water is transparent, which means that light can pass through it. This is important for organisms that live in water, because most of them need sunlight to make food.

Chemical Structure of Water

To understand some of water's properties, you need to know more about its chemical structure. As you have seen, each molecule of water consists of one atom of oxygen and two atoms of hydrogen. The oxygen atom in a water molecule attracts negatively-charged electrons more strongly than the hydrogen atoms do. As a result, the oxygen atom has a slightly negative charge, and the hydrogen atoms have a slightly positive charge. A difference in electrical charge between different parts of the same molecule is called polarity, making water a polar molecule. The diagram in Figure to the right shows water's polarity.

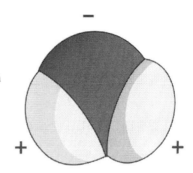

Water Molecule. This diagram shows the positive and negative parts of a water molecule.

Opposites attract when it comes to charged molecules. In the case of water, the positive (hydrogen) end of one water molecule is attracted to the negative (oxygen) end of a nearby water molecule. Because of this attraction, weak bonds form between adjacent water molecules, as shown in the diagram to the left. This type of bond that forms between molecules is called a hydrogen bond. Bonds between molecules are not as strong as bonds within molecules, but in water they are strong enough to hold together nearby molecules.

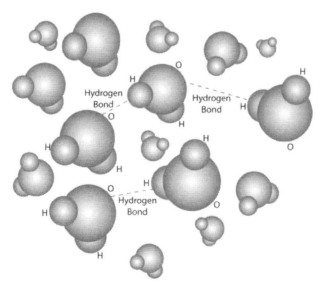

Hydrogen Bonding in Water Molecules. Hydrogen bonds form between nearby water molecules. How do you think this might affect water's properties?

Properties of Water

Hydrogen bonds between water molecules explain some of water's properties. For example, hydrogen bonds explain why water molecules tend to stick together or have cohesion. Hydrogen bonds are constantly breaking, with new bonds being formed with different molecules. Have you ever watched water drip from a leaky faucet or from a melting icicle? If you have, then you know that water always falls in drops rather than as separate molecules. The dew drops in the diagram below are another example of water molecules sticking together. Water also has high adhesion properties (the ability of water molecules to be attracted to other substances) because of its polar nature. On extremely clean/smooth glass the water may form a thin film because the molecular forces between glass and water molecules (adhesive forces) are stronger than the cohesive forces.

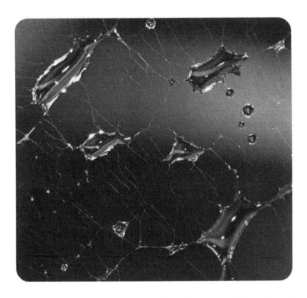

Droplets of Dew. Drops of dew cling to a spider web in this picture. Can you think of other examples of water forming drops? (Hint: What happens when rain falls on a newly waxed car?

Hydrogen bonds cause water to have a relatively high boiling point of 100°C (212°F). Because of its high boiling point, most water on Earth is in a liquid state rather than in a gaseous state. Water in its liquid state is needed by all living things. Hydrogen bonds also cause water to form into a crystalline type structure thus expanding when it freezes. This, in turn, causes ice to have a lower density (mass/volume) than liquid water. The lower density of ice means that it floats on water. For example, in cold climates, ice floats on top of the water in lakes. This allows lake animals such as fish to survive the winter by staying in the liquid water under the ice.

Water as the Universal Solvent

Due to hydrogen bonds, water dissolves more substances than any other common liquid. Most elements have high solubilities in water, which means that even in large concentrations, many things will dissolve into and be suspended in water.

The figure to the right shows salt a crystal being dissolved by water, individual ions hydrated. *Source: universe-review.ca*

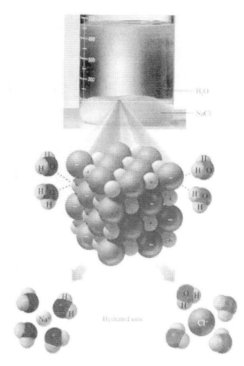

Three States of Water

Water is the only substance on Earth that is present in all three states of matter – as a solid, liquid or gas. (And Earth is the only planet where water is present in all three states.) Because of the ranges in temperature in specific locations around the planet, all three phases may be present in a single location or in a region. The three phases are solid (ice or snow), liquid (water), and gas (water vapor). See ice, water, and clouds (Figure below).

(a) Ice floating in the sea. Can you find all three phases of water in this image? (b) Liquid water. (c) Water vapor is invisible, but clouds that form when water vapor condenses are not.

SUMMARY

- Water is a polar molecule with a more positive charge on one side and a more negative charge on the other side.
- Water is the only substance on Earth that is stable in all three states.
- Earth is the only planet in the Solar System that has water in all three states.
- Some special properties of water are cohesion (the ability to stick to itself) and adhesion (the ability to stick to other substances).

Review Questions

5. List three unique properties that water has due to hydrogen bonding?

6. Water can exist in all three states of matter. Why is water typically in the liquid form?

7. Why is it essential for life that water is less dense when frozen than when liquid?

8. Water always beads up on a freshly waxed car. Is this due to adhesion or cohesion? Both? Explain.

9. Why is water considered a polar molecule?

THE DISTRIBUTION OF WATER ON EARTH

Lesson Objectives

- Describe how water is distributed on Earth.
- Describe what powers the water cycle and how water moves through this cycle.

Introduction

Water is simply two atoms of hydrogen and one atom of oxygen bonded together. Despite its simplicity, water has remarkable properties. Water expands when it freezes, has high surface tension (because of the polar nature of the molecules, they tend to stick together), and others. Without water, life might not be able to exist on Earth and it certainly would not have the tremendous complexity and diversity that we see.

Distribution of Earth's Water

Earth's oceans contain 97% of the planet's water, so just 3% is fresh water, water with low concentrations of salts (See diagram below). Most fresh water is trapped as ice in the vast glaciers and ice sheets of Greenland. A storage location for water such as an ocean, glacier, ground water, lakes, or even the atmosphere is known as a reservoir. A water molecule may pass through a reservoir very quickly or may remain for much longer. The amount of time a molecule stays in a reservoir is known as its residence time.

How is the 3% of fresh water divided into different reservoirs? How much of that water is useful for living creatures? How much is available for people?

Distribution of Water on Earth

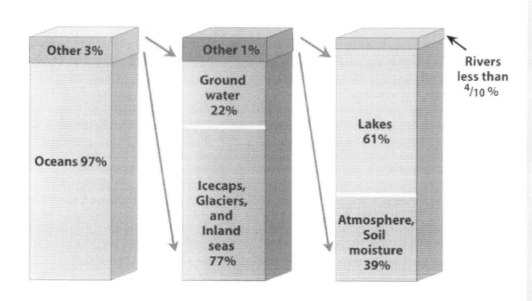

Vocabulary

- condensation
- evaporation
- fresh water
- groundwater
- hydrologic (water) cycle
- precipitation
- natural purification
- reservoir
- residence time
- sublimation
- transpiration
- water vapor

163

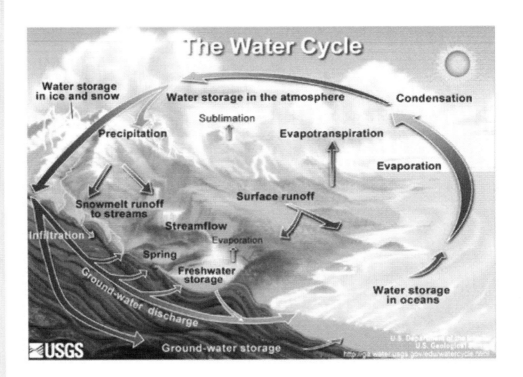

The Hydrologic (Water) Cycle

Because of the unique properties of water, water molecules can cycle through almost anywhere on Earth. The water molecule found in your glass of water today could have erupted from a volcano early in Earth history. In the intervening billions of years, the molecule probably spent time in a glacier or far below the ground. The molecule surely was high up in the atmosphere and maybe deep in the belly of a dinosaur. Where will that water molecule go next?

Because Earth's water is present in all three states, it can get into a variety of environments around the planet. The movement of water around Earth's surface is the hydrologic (water) cycle (Figure above).

Because it is a cycle, the water cycle has no beginning and no end. It has been an ongoing process since well before the dinosaurs.

The Sun, many millions of kilometers away, provides the energy that drives the water cycle. Our nearest star directly impacts the water cycle by supplying the energy needed for evaporation.

Most of Earth's water is stored in the oceans where it can remain for hundreds or thousands of years. The oceans are discussed in detail in the chapter Earth's Oceans.

Water changes from a liquid to a gas by evaporation to become water vapor. The Sun's energy can evaporate water from the ocean surface or from lakes, streams, or puddles on land. Only the water molecules evaporate; the salts remain in the ocean or a fresh water reservoir.

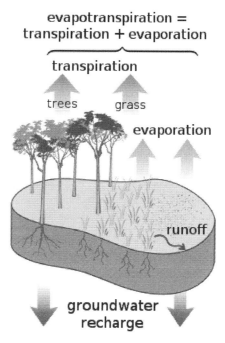

The water vapor remains in the atmosphere until it undergoes condensation to become tiny droplets of liquid. The droplets gather in clouds, which are blown about the globe by wind. As the water droplets in the clouds collide and grow, they fall from the sky as precipitation. Precipitation can be rain, sleet, hail, or snow. Sometimes precipitation falls into the ocean and sometimes it falls onto the land surface.

When water falls from the sky as rain it may enter streams and rivers that flow downward to oceans and lakes. Water that falls as snow may sit on a mountain for several months. Snow may become part of the ice in a glacier, where it may remain for hundreds or thousands of years. Snow and ice may go directly back into the air by sublimation, the process in which a solid changes directly into a gas without first becoming a liquid. Although you probably have not seen water vapor sublimating from a glacier, you may have seen dry ice sublimate in air.

Snow and ice slowly melt over time to become liquid water. This provides a steady flow of fresh water to streams, rivers, and lakes below. A water droplet falling as rain could also become part of a stream or a lake. At the surface, the water may eventually evaporate and reenter the atmosphere.

A significant amount of water infiltrates into the ground. Soil moisture is an important reservoir for water. Water trapped in soil is important for plants to grow. Water may seep through dirt and rock below the soil through pores infiltrating the ground to go into Earth's groundwater system. Groundwater enters aquifers that may store fresh water for centuries. Alternatively, the water may come to the surface through springs or find its way back to the oceans.

Plants and animals depend on water to live and they also play a role in the water cycle. Plants take up water from the soil and release large amounts of water vapor into the air through their leaves (Figure to the right), a process known as transpiration. As water moves between each stage in the water cycle, water undergoes natural purification. Sediments and pollutants are filtered out as water moves between layers of soil. As water evaporates, other non-water and various contaminants are left behind. This natural cycling helps to purify water and has been copied, in part, to modern innovation in our water treatment facilities.

Clouds form above the Amazon Rainforest even in the dry season
because of moisture from plant transpiration.

People also depend on water as a natural resource. Not content to get water directly from streams or ponds, humans create canals, aqueducts, dams, and wells to collect water and direct it to where they want it.

Water Use		
Use	United States	Global
Agriculture	34%	70%
Domestic (drinking, bathing)	12%	10%
Industry	5%	20%
Power plant cooling	49%	small

Table 1.1 above displays water use in the United States and globally (Estimated Use of Water in the United States in 2005, USGS).

It is important to note that water molecules cycle around. If climate cools and glaciers and ice caps grow, there is less water for the oceans and sea level will fall. The reverse can also happen.

LESSON SUMMARY

- Although Earth's surface is mostly water covered, only 3% is fresh water.
- Water travels between phases and reservoirs as part of the hydrologic (water) cycle.
- The major processes of the water cycle include evaporation, transpiration, condensation, precipitation, and return to the oceans via runoff and groundwater supplies.

Review Questions

1. About what percent of the Earth's water is fresh water?
2. In what states does water appear on Earth and on other planets?
3. What powers the water cycle? How?
4. In which of the states of matter would water be at 130oC? At 45oC?
5. Define the words condensation and evaporation.
6. Sketch the water cycle.
7. What is transpiration? How is it like evaporation?

Points to Consider

- What natural disasters are caused by the water cycle?
- As Earth's temperature warms, how might the water cycle be altered?

Going Further

An online guide to the hydrologic cycle from the University of Illinois is found here:
http://ww2010.atmos.uiuc.edu/%28Gh%29/guides/mtr/hyd/home.rxml

This animation shows the annual cycle of monthly mean precipitation around the world:
http://en.wikipedia.org/wiki/File:MeanMonthlyP.gif

WATER RESERVOIRS

Lesson Objectives
- Define groundwater.
- Explain the location, use, and importance of aquifers.
- Define springs and geysers.
- Describe how wells work and why they are important.

Introduction
Although this may seem surprising, water beneath the ground is commonplace. Usually groundwater travels slowly and silently beneath the surface, but in some locations it bubbles to the surface at springs and geysers. The products of erosion and deposition by groundwater were described in the Erosion and Deposition chapter.

Groundwater
Groundwater is the largest reservoir of liquid fresh water on Earth and is found in aquifers, porous rock and sediment with water in between. Water is attracted to the soil particles and capillary action, which describes how water moves through a porous media, moves water from wet soil to dry areas.

Aquifers are found at different depths. Some are just below the surface and some are found much deeper below the land surface. A region may have more than one aquifer beneath it and even most deserts are above aquifers. The source region for an aquifer beneath a desert is likely to be far from where the aquifer is located; for example, it may be in a mountain area.

The amount of water that is available to enter groundwater in a region is influenced by the local climate, the slope of the land, the type of rock found at the surface, the vegetation cover, land use in the area, and water retention, which is the amount of water that remains in the ground. More water goes into the ground where there is a lot of rain, flat land, porous rock, exposed soil, and where water is not already filling the soil and rock.

The residence time of water in a groundwater aquifer can be from minutes to thousands of years. Groundwater is often called "fossil water" because it has remained in the ground for so long, often since the end of the ice ages.

Vocabulary
- aquifer
- capillary action
- impermeable
- permeability
- porosity
- subsidence
- water table
- well
- abiotic factor
- biotic factor

Aquifers

An aquifer is an underground layer of rock that is saturated with groundwater. To be a good aquifer, the rock in the aquifer must have good:

- **porosity: small spaces between grains**
- **permeability: connections between pores**

To reach an aquifer, surface water infiltrates downward into the ground through tiny spaces or pores in the rock. The water travels down through the permeable rock until it reaches a layer that does not have pores; this rock is impermeable (Figure below). This impermeable rock layer forms the base of the aquifer. The upper surface where the groundwater reaches is the water table.

The Water Table

For a groundwater aquifer to contain the same amount of water, the amount of recharge must equal the amount of discharge. What are the likely sources of recharge? What are the likely sources of discharge?

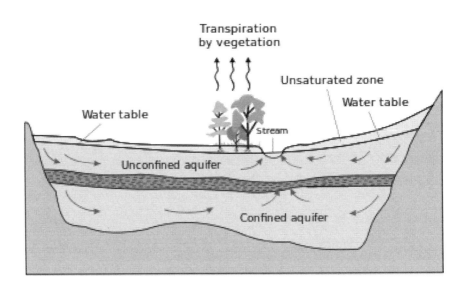

In wet regions, streams are fed by groundwater; the surface of the stream is the top of the water table (Figure below). In dry regions, water seeps down from the stream into the aquifer. These streams are often dry much of the year. Water leaves a groundwater reservoir in streams or springs. People take water from aquifers, too.

What happens to the water table when there is a lot of rainfall? What happens when there is a drought? Although groundwater levels do not rise and fall as rapidly as at the surface, over time the water table will rise during wet periods and fall during droughts.

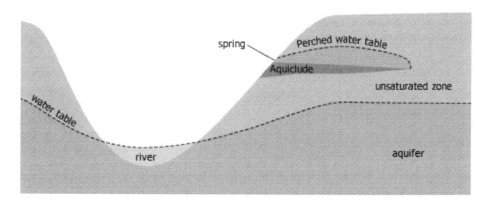

The top of the stream is the top of the water table. The stream feeds the aquifer. If the stream level changes, the level of the aquifer will change along with it.

Groundwater Use

Groundwater is an extremely important water source for people. Groundwater is a renewable resource and its use is sustainable when the water pumped from the aquifer is replenished. It is important for anyone who intends to dig a well to know how deep beneath the surface the water table is. Because groundwater involves interaction between the Earth and the water, the study of groundwater is called hydrogeology.

Some aquifers are overused; people pump out more water than is replaced. As the water is pumped out, the water table slowly falls, requiring wells to be dug deeper, which takes more money and energy. Wells may go completely dry if they are not deep enough to reach into the lowered water table.

Lowering the water table may cause the ground surface to sink. Subsidence may occur beneath houses and other structures (Figure to the left). This picture depicts levels how far the ground has sunk since 1925 till current day in the San Jaoquin valley of California.

When coastal aquifers are overused, salt water from the ocean may enter the aquifer, contaminating the aquifer and making it less useful for drinking and irrigation. Salt water incursion is a problem in developed coastal regions, such as on Hawaii.

Wells

A well is created by digging or drilling to reach groundwater. When the water table is close to the surface, wells are a convenient method for extracting water. When the water table is far below the surface, specialized equipment must be used to dig a well. Most wells use motorized pumps to bring water to the surface, but some still require people to use a bucket to draw water up.

LESSON SUMMARY

- Groundwater is the largest reservoir of fresh water.
- The water table is the top of an aquifer below which is water and above is rock or soil mixed with air.
- Aquifers are underground areas of sediment or rock that hold groundwater.
- An aquifer needs good porosity and permeability.
- People dig or drill wells to access groundwater.

Review Questions

1. What is groundwater?
2. What is the water table?
3. What are aquifers and why are they so important?
4. What is groundwater recharge? what factors influence the rate of recharge?
5. How does a well work?
6. Since groundwater is largely unseen from the surface, how might you monitor the amount of groundwater in an aquifer?

Critical Thinking

There are many factors that can influence freshwater ecosystems. Below is a list of both biotic and abiotic factors that can play a role, some good some bad. Biotic factors are living factors that affect an ecosystem, whereas abiotic factors are non-living factors that affect ecosystems. Cite specific examples of how each of the factors below can influence a freshwater ecosystem. Lastly, come up with at least one biotic and abiotic factor not included in the list and explain how they can impact the water systems as well.

Biotic factors:
Predator Prey Relationships
Algae Growth
Plant/Animal Concentrations

Abiotic factors:
Dissolved Oxygen Content
Sunlight
Nutrient/fertilizer input
Dams

Points to Consider

Is water from a river or from a well more likely to be clean to drink?
Why is overuse of groundwater a big concern?
What policies might people put in place to conserve water levels in lakes and aquifers

Going Further

This animation shows porosity and permeability. The water droplets are found in the pores between the sediment grains, which is porosity. When the water can travel between ores, that's permeability.
http://www.nature.nps.gov/GEOLOGY/usgsnps/animate/POROS_3.MPG

Vocabulary

o   drought

o   irrigation

HUMAN WATER USE

Lesson Objectives

- List ways that humans use water.
- State why some people don't have enough water.
- Explain why poor quality water is a problem.

Introduction

All forms of life need water to survive. Humans are no exception. We can survive for only a few days without it. We also need water for agriculture, industry, and many other uses. Clearly, water is one of Earth's most important natural resources. It's a good thing that water is recycled in the water cycle.

HOW WE USE WATER

Water in Agriculture

Many crops are grown where there isn't enough rainfall for plants to thrive. For example, crops are grown in deserts of the American, such as Utah. How is this possible? The answer is irrigation. Irrigation is any way of providing extra water to plants. Most of the water used in agriculture is used for irrigation. Livestock also use water, but they use much less.

Irrigation can waste a lot of water. The type of irrigation shown in the image below is the most wasteful. The water is simply sprayed into the air. Then it falls to the ground like rain. But much of the water never reaches the crops. Instead, it evaporates in the air or runs off the fields. Irrigation water may dissolve agricultural chemicals such as fertilizer. The dissolved chemicals could soak into groundwater or run off into rivers or lakes. Salts in irrigation water can also collect in the soil. The soil may get too salty for plants to grow.

Overhead irrigation systems like this one are widely used to irrigate crops on big farms. What are some drawbacks of irrigation?

Water in Industry

Almost a quarter of the water used worldwide is used in industry. Industries use water for many purposes. For example, they may use water to cool machines. Or they may use it in chemical processes. These uses of water may pollute it. Water is also used to generate electricity. This use doesn't pollute the water. But it may dam up streams and rivers. This can harm wildlife.

Household Uses of Water

Think about all the ways people use water at home. Besides drinking it, they use it for cooking, bathing, washing dishes, doing laundry, and flushing toilets. The water used inside homes goes down the drain. It usually ends up in a sewer system. This water can be treated and reused.

Households may also use water outdoors. If your family has a lawn or garden, you may water them with a hose or sprinkler. You may also use water to wash the car. Much of the water used outdoors evaporates or runs off. The runoff water may end up in storm sewers. They carry it to a body of water, such as the ocean.

Water for Fun

There are many ways to use water for fun, from white water rafting to snorkeling. These uses of water don't actually use water up. If you were to guess which recreational activity consumes the most water, what would you guess? Believe it or not, it's golf! Playing golf doesn't use water, but keeping golf courses green uses a lot of water. Many golf courses have sprinkler systems. They keep the greens well watered. Much of this water is wasted. It evaporates or runs off the ground.

Water Problems: Not Enough Water

Most Americans have plenty of fresh, clean water. But many people around the world do not. In fact, water scarcity is the world's most serious resource problem. How can that be? Water is almost everywhere. More than 70 percent of Earth's surface is covered by water.

Where Is All the Water?

One problem is that only a tiny fraction of Earth's water is fresh, liquid water that people can use. More than 97 percent of Earth's water is salt water in the oceans. Just 3 percent of all water on earth is freshwater. Most of the freshwater is frozen in ice sheets, icebergs, and glaciers (see Figure below).

This glacier in Patagonia, Argentina stores a lot of frozen freshwater

Rainfall and the Water Supply

Rainfall varies around the globe. About 40 percent of the land gets very little rain. About the same percentage of the world's people don't have enough water. Drier climates generally have less water for people to use. In some places, people may have less water for an entire year than many Americans use in a single day! How much water is there where you live?

Wealth and the Water Supply

Richer nations can drill deep wells or supply people with water in other ways. In these countries, just about everyone has access to clean running water in their homes. It's no surprise that people in these countries also use the most water. In poorer nations, there is little money to develop water supplies.

Water Shortages

Water shortages are common in much of the world. They are most likely during droughts. A drought is a period of unusually low rainfall. Human actions have increased how often droughts occur. One way is by cutting down trees. Trees add a lot of water vapor to the air through transpiration. With fewer trees, the air is drier and droughts are more common.

We already use six times as much water today as we did a hundred years ago. As the number of people rises, our need for water will grow. By the year 2025, only half the world's people will have enough. Water is such a vital resource that serious water shortages may cause other problems:

- Crops and livestock may die so people will have nothing to eat.
- Other uses of water, such as industry, may have to stop.
- People may fight over water resources.
- People may die from lack of water.

Water Problems: Poor Quality Water

The water Americans get from their faucets is generally safe. This water has been treated and purified. But at least 20 percent of the world's people do not have clean drinking water. Their only choice may be to drink water straight from a river (see image below). The river water may be polluted with wastes. It may contain bacteria and other organisms that cause disease. Almost 9 out of 10 cases of disease worldwide are caused by unsafe drinking water. It's the leading cause of death in young children.

This boy is getting drinking water from a hole that has been dug. It may be the only source of water where he lives.

LESSON SUMMARY

- People use water for agriculture, industry, and municipal uses. Agriculture uses the most water. Almost all of it goes for irrigation.
- Too little water is a major problem. Places with the least water get little rainfall. They also lack money to develop water resources. Droughts make the problem even worse.
- Poor water quality is also a problem. Many people must drink water that contains wastes. This causes a lot of illness and death.

Lesson Review Questions

1. List the three major ways that humans use water.
2. What is the single biggest use of water in agriculture?
3. Give an example of an industrial use of water.
4. What problems may result from serious water shortages?
5. More than 70 percent of Earth's surface is covered by water. Why is scarcity of water the world's most serious resource problem?

Points to Consider

- In this lesson, you learned that many people don't have clean water to drink. They must drink polluted water instead.
- How does water become polluted?
- Can polluted water be treated so it is safe to drink?

WATER POLLUTION

Lesson Objectives

- Define point and nonpoint source pollution.
- List sources of water pollution.
- Describe ocean water pollution.
- Identify causes and effects of thermal pollution.

Introduction
Water pollution is a worldwide problem. Almost anything can end up in Earth's water.

Point and Nonpoint Source Pollution
Pollution that enters water at just one point is called point source pollution. For example, chemicals from a factory might empty into a stream through a single pipe (see Figure below). Pollution that enters in many places is called nonpoint source pollution. It happens when runoff carries pollution into a body of water. Which type of pollution do you think is harder to control? .

Sources of Water Pollution
There are three main sources of water pollution:

- Agriculture
- Industry
- Municipal, or community, sources.

Water Pollution from Agriculture
Huge amounts of chemicals such as fertilizer are applied to farm fields. The chemicals dissolve in rainwater. Runoff may carry some of the chemicals to nearby rivers or lakes. Dissolved fertilizer causes too much growth of water plants and algae. This can lead to dead zones in the water where nothing can live. Also, some of the chemicals may soak into the ground and pollute groundwater. They may end up in water wells. If people drink the polluted water, they may get sick. Waste (fecal matter) from livestock can also pollute water. The waste contains bacteria and other organisms that cause disease. In fact, more than 40 human diseases can be caused by water polluted with animal waste. Many farms in the U.S. have thousands of animals. They produce millions of gallons of waste.

The waste is stored in huge lagoons. Many leaks have occurred. Two examples are described below.

- In North Carolina, 25 million gallons of hog manure spilled into a nearby river. It killed millions of fish.
- In Wisconsin, cow manure leaked into a city's water supply. Almost half a million people got sick. More than 100 of them died.

Water Pollution from Industry

- Factories and power plants may pollute water with harmful substances.
- Many industries produce toxic chemicals. Some of the worst are arsenic, lead, and mercury.
- Nuclear power plants produce radioactive chemicals. They cause cancer and other serious health problems.
- Oil tanks and pipelines can leak. Leaks may not be noticed until a lot of oil has soaked into the ground. The oil may pollute groundwater so it is no longer fit to drink.

Municipal Water Pollution

"Municipal" refers to the community. Households and businesses in a community may also pollute the water supply. For example:

- People apply chemicals to their lawns. The chemicals dissolve in rainwater. They run off into storm sewers and end up in nearby rivers or lakes.
- Underground septic tanks can develop leaks. They let household sewage seep into groundwater.
- Municipal sewage treatment plants dump treated wastewater into rivers or lakes. The wastewater may not be treated enough. It may still contain bacteria or toxic chemicals.

Ocean Water Pollution

The oceans are vast. You might think they are too big to be harmed by pollution. But that's not the case. Ocean water is becoming seriously polluted.

Coastal Pollution

The oceans are most polluted along coasts. That's because pollution usually enters ocean water from land. Runoff and rivers carry the majority of pollution into the ocean. Many cities also dump their wastewater there. In some parts of the world, raw sewage and trash may be thrown into the water. Coastal water may become so polluted that people get sick if they swim in it or eat seafood from it. The polluted water may also kill fish and other ocean life.

Oil Spills

Oil spills are another source of ocean pollution. Many oil rigs float on the oceans. They pump oil from beneath the ocean floor. Huge ocean tankers also carry oil around the world. Millions of barrels of oil may end up in the water if anything goes wrong. The oil may coat and kill ocean animals. Much of the oil may wash ashore. It can destroy coastal wetlands and ruin beaches. The figure to the left shows oil on a Louisiana beach after an oil spill. The oil washed ashore after a deadly oil rig explosion in the Gulf of Mexico in 2010.

After an oil rig explosion, hundreds of miles of beaches looked like this one. Cleaning them up was a huge task.

Thermal Pollution

Thermal pollution is pollution that raises the temperature of water. It's commonly caused by power plants and factories. They use cold water to cool their machines. They may pump cold water from a lake through giant cooling towers, like those in the Figure below. The cold water absorbs heat as it flows through the towers. Then the warm water is returned to the lake. It can kill fish and other water life. One reason is that warm water can't hold as much oxygen as cool water. It may not have enough oxygen for living things.

Nuclear power plants need huge amounts of water for cooling, so they are built close to water. The water that's returned to the lake may be warm enough to kill fish.

LESSON SUMMARY

- Point source pollution enters water at just one place. For example, it might enter a stream through a pipe. Nonpoint source pollution enters water everywhere. It is carried by runoff.
- Major sources of pollution are agriculture, industry, and communities. Pollution from agriculture includes chemicals and animal waste. Industry produces toxic chemicals. Communities produce sewage.
- Ocean water is most polluted along coasts. That's because pollution usually enters the water from land. Oil spills also pollute ocean water.
- Thermal pollution raises the temperature of water. It is commonly caused by power plants and factories. The change in temperature can kill fish and other water organisms.

Lesson Review Questions

1. Describe two major ways that agriculture can pollute water.
2. List 3 harmful substances that industry may add to water.
3. What are three municipal sources of water pollution?
4. State why ocean water is most polluted near coasts.
5. Name 2 ways oil can end up in ocean water?
6. What is thermal pollution? Why is it harmful for fish and other water life?
7. A nuclear power plant is located near the ocean. The plant uses ocean water for cooling. Describe two types of water pollution this plant might produce.
8. Compare and contrast point and nonpoint source pollution. Give an example of each.

Points to Consider

- People can't live without water. They need it for life itself. More than almost any other resource, water must be protected.
- How can water pollution be prevented?
- How can we use less water?

POLLUTION PREVENTION

Lesson Objectives

- List ways to reduce water pollution.
- Describe how water is treated.
- Identify ways to conserve water.

Introduction

The water supply can be harmed in two major ways. It can be polluted, and it can be overused. Protecting the water supply must address both problems. We need to reduce how much pollution ends up in the water supply. We need to treat water that's already polluted. We need to conserve water by using less.

Reducing Water Pollution

In the mid 1900s, people were startled to see the Cuyahoga River in Cleveland, Ohio, burst into flames! The river was so polluted with oil and other industrial wastes that it was flammable. Nothing could live in it.

Controlling Water Pollution

Disasters such as rivers burning led to new U.S. laws to protect the water. For example, the Environmental Protection Agency was established. The Clean Water Act was passed. Now, water is routinely tested. Pollution is tracked to its source, and polluters are fined. They also must fix the problem and clean up the pollution. Industries, agriculture, and communities may still pollute water, but much less than before.

What You Can Do

Most water pollution comes from industry, agriculture, and municipal sources. But even individuals can pollute the water supply if they aren't careful. What can you do to reduce water pollution? Read the tips below. Properly dispose of motor oil and household chemicals. Never pour them down the drain. Also, don't let them spill on the ground. This keeps them out of storm sewers and bodies of water.

Use fewer lawn and garden chemicals. Use natural products instead. For example, use compost instead of fertilizer. Or grow plants that can thrive on their own without any extra help.

Repair engine oil leaks right away. A steady drip of oil from an engine can quickly add up to gallons. The oil can wash off driveways and streets. It can end up in storm drains and pollute the water supply.

Don't let pet litter or pet wastes get into the water supply. The nitrogen they contain can cause overgrowth of algae. The wastes may also contain bacteria and other causes of disease.

Water Treatment

Water treatment is a series of processes that remove unwanted substances from water. It makes water safe to return to the natural environment or to the human water supply. You can see how drinking water is treated in the Figure to the left. Treating water for other purposes may not include all the same steps. That's because water used in agriculture or industry may not have to be as clean as drinking water.

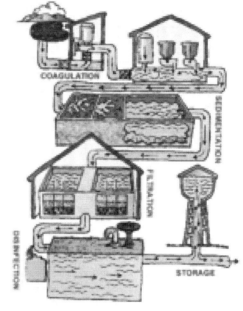

Four processes are used to treat water to make it safe for drinking.

Conserving Water

Conserving water means using less of it. This applies mostly to people in richer nations. They have the most water and also waste the most. In other countries, people already use very little water. They can't get by with less.

Saving Water in Irrigation

Irrigation is the single biggest use of water. Overhead irrigation wastes a lot of water. Drip irrigation wastes less. Water pipes run over the surface of the ground. There are tiny holes in the pipes close to each plant. Water slowly drips out of the holes and soaks into the soil around the plants. Less water is needed. Very little of it evaporates or runs off the ground.

Rationing Water

Some communities save water with rationing. They ban the use of water for certain things. For example, they may ban lawn watering and car washing. People may be fined if they use water in these ways. You can do your part. Follow any bans where you live. They are most likely to apply during droughts.

Saving Water at Home

It's easy to save water at home. You can save water every day of the year. Saving even a few gallons a day can make a big difference over the long run. The best place to start saving water is in the bathroom. Toilet flushing is the single biggest use of water in the home. Showers and baths are the next biggest use. Follow the tips below to save water at home.

Install water-saving toilets. They use only about half as much water per flush. A single household can save up to 20,000 gallons a year with this change alone!
Take shorter showers. You can get just as clean in 5 minutes as you can in 10. And you'll save up to 50 gallons of water each time you shower. That's thousands of gallons each year.

Use low-flow shower heads. They use about half as much water as regular shower heads. They save thousands of gallons of water.

Fix leaky shower heads and faucets. All those drips really add up. At one drip per second, more than 6,000 gallons go down the drain in a year — per faucet!

Don't leave the water running while you brush your teeth. You could save as much as 10 gallons each time you brush. That could add up to 10,000 gallons in a year.

Landscape the home with plants that need little water. This could result in a huge savings in water use. Look at the garden in the Figure below. It shows that you don't have to sacrifice beauty to save water.

This beautiful garden contains only plants that need very little water.

186

LESSON SUMMARY

- Laws have been passed to control water pollution. In many places, water is cleaner now than it used to be. Everyone can help reduce water pollution. For example, they can keep motor oil and pet wastes out of the water supply.
- Water treatment is a series of processes that remove unwanted substances from water.
- More processes are needed to purify water for drinking than for other uses.
- There are many ways to use less water. For example, drip irrigation wastes less than other methods. Water-saving toilets and shower heads can save a lot of water at home.

Lesson Review Questions

1. Identify three ways that people can reduce water pollution at home.
2. List the processes used to treat drinking water.
3. What is filtration? What does it remove from water?
4. Why is chlorine added to drinking water?
5. Describe how water might be rationed in a community. Why would this be done?
6. What are some of the unique properties of water that make it so important to life?
7. Where is water found on Earth? What percentage of Earth's water is located in each reservoir?
8. Approximately how much of Earth's water is freshwater? What percentage of Earth's freshwater is located in each reservoir?
9. Sketch and label the Hydrologic (water) cycle.
10. What is the energy source for the hydrologic cycle?
11. What sorts of natural disasters could be caused by the hydrologic cycle?
12. List the four major ways water is used by humans. How is water used differently in the United States compared to the rest of the world?
13. What makes certain kinds of rock good aquifers?
14. Define water table. Why is it important to monitor the water table?
15. Why is water shortage such a concern in our area?
16. What are the 3 main sources of water pollution?
17. Why is thermal pollution a problem?
18. What is the difference between point source and non-point source pollution?
19. Describe 3 things you can do to help reduce water pollution.
20. Explain the water treatment process, and why each of the 5 steps is important.
21. List 5 ways you can conserve water at home.

STANDARD 4, OBJECTIVE 2. ANALYZE THE CHARACTERISTICS AND IMPORTANCE OF FRESHWATER FOUND ON EARTH'S SURFACE AND ITS EFFECT ON LIVING SYSTEMS.

States of Water

H - two - O. Why is something so simple so important?

Water is the most important substance on Earth. Think about all the things you use water for? If your water access were restricted what would you miss about it?

The Water Molecule

Water is simply two atoms of hydrogen and one atom of oxygen bonded together. The hydrogen ions are on one side of the oxygen ion, making water a **polar molecule**. This means that one side, the side with the hydrogen ions, has a slightly positive electrical charge. The other side, the side without the hydrogen ions, has a slightly negative charge.

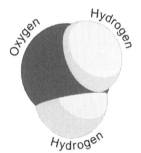

A water molecule. The hydrogen atoms have a slightly positive charge, and the oxygen atom has a slightly negative charge.

Despite its simplicity, water has remarkable properties. Water expands when it freezes, has high surface tension (because of the polar nature of the molecules, they tend to stick together), and others. Without water, life might not be able to exist on Earth and it certainly would not have the tremendous complexity and diversity that we see.

Three States of Matter

Water is the only substance on Earth that is present in all three states of matter – as a solid, liquid or gas. (And Earth is the only planet where water is present in all three states.) Because of the ranges in temperature in specific locations around the planet, all three phases may be present in a single location or in a region. The three phases are solid (ice or snow), liquid (water), and gas (**water vapor**). See ice, water, and clouds (**Figure** opposite).

188

(a) Ice floating in the sea. Can you find all three phases of water in this image? (b) Liquid water. (c) Water vapor is invisible, but clouds that form when water vapor condenses are not.

SUMMARY

- Water is a polar molecule with a more positive charge on one side and a more negative charge on the other side.
- Water is the only substance on Earth that is stable in all three states.
- Earth is the only planet in the Solar System that has water in all three states.

PRACTICE

Use this resource to answer the questions that follow.

http://www.youtube.com/watch?v=KCL8zqjXbME

1. What is water made of?
2. Explain how water becomes a solid.
3. What happens when a solid melts?
4. How do molecules move in a liquid?
5. What are the major differences between a solid, a liquid, and a gas?

REVIEW

6. What is a polar molecule?
7. What are the three states that a substance can have?
8. Where in the solar system is water found in all three states?

FRESHWATER AND WETLANDS BIOMES

What may be the most biologically diverse type of ecosystem?

These are wetland marshes in eastern Finland. Notice the abundance of vegetation mixed with the water. And of course, where there are plants, there are animals. Wetlands are considered the most biologically diverse of all ecosystems. Plant life found in wetlands includes mangrove, water lilies, cattails, black spruce, cypress, and many others. Animal life includes many different amphibians, reptiles, birds, insects, and mammals.

Freshwater Biomes

Freshwater biomes have water that contains little or no salt. They include standing and running freshwater biomes. Standing freshwater biomes include ponds and lakes. Lakes are generally bigger and deeper than ponds. Some of the water in lakes is in the aphotic zone, where there is too little sunlight for photosynthesis. Plankton and plants, such as the duckweed in the **Figure** opposite, are the primary producers in standing freshwater biomes.

Freshwater Producers

Duckweed in a pond   Cattails in a stream

The pond on the left has a thick mat of duckweed plants. They cover the surface of the water and use sunlight for photosynthesis. The cattails on the right grow along a stream bed. They have tough, slender leaves that can withstand moving water.

Running freshwater biomes include streams and rivers. Rivers are usually larger than streams. Streams may start with runoff or water seeping out of a spring. The water runs downhill and joins other running water to become a stream. A stream may flow into a river that empties into a lake or the ocean. Running water is better able to dissolve oxygen and nutrients than standing water. However, the moving water is a challenge to many living things. Algae and plants, such as the cattails in **the Figure above**, are the primary producers in running water biomes.

WETLANDS

A **wetland** is an area that is saturated with water or covered by water for at least one season of the year. The water may be freshwater or salt water. Wetlands are extremely important biomes for several reasons:

- They store excess water from floods.
- They slow down runoff and help prevent erosion.
- They remove excess nutrients from runoff before it empties into rivers or lakes.
- They provide a unique habitat that certain communities of plants need to survive.
- They provide a safe, lush habitat for many species of animals, so they have high biodiversity.

See *Biomes: Wetlands* at http://www.neok12.com/php/watch.php?v=zX03547a4151505c53040173&t=Ecosystems and *Biomes: Freshwater* at http://www.neok12.com/php/watch.php?v=zX466d047304046105745367&t=Ecosystems for additional information.

RESTORING WETLANDS

More than 100,000 acres of wetlands are being restored in the Northern California Bay Area, but how exactly do we know what to restore them to? Historical ecologists are recreating San Francisco Bay wetlands that existed decades ago. To learn more, see http://www.kqed.org/quest/television/view/416.

For more than 100 years, south San Francisco Bay has been a center for industrial salt production. Now federal and state biologists are working to restore the ponds to healthy wetlands for fish and other wildlife. Salt marshes are rich habitats that provide shelter and food for many species, some of which are endangered or threatened. For additional information, see:
http://www.kqed.org/quest/television/from-salt-ponds-to-wetlands

SAN FRANCISCO BAY: A UNIQUE ESTUARY

An **estuary** is a partly enclosed coastal body of water with one or more rivers or streams flowing into it, and with a free connection to the ocean. Estuaries can be thought of as the most biologically productive regions on Earth, with very high biodiversity. Estuaries are zones where land and sea come together, and where fresh and salt water meet. The San Francisco Bay is one of the great estuaries of the world. For additional information, see:
http://www.youtube.com/watch?v=clZz20jE5nO&playnext=1&list=PL0AAA2B9B3E9F6AB3

SUMMARY

- Freshwater biomes include standing water and running water biomes.
- Wetlands are extremely important biomes. They may have freshwater or salt water.

PRACTICE

Use this resource to answer the questions that follow.
http://www.hippocampus.org/Biology → Non-Majors Biology → Search:Freshwater Biomes

1. Why are freshwater biomes considered "limited"?
2. Describe a wetland. Give examples of wetlands.
3. What are the 3 zones of ponds and lakes?
4. Compare the littoral zone to the profundal zone.
5. What types of organisms can thrive in the headwaters of streams and rivers?
6. Describe the changes that occur when a river empties into a lake or ocean.

REVIEW

9. Describe a freshwater biome.
10. Define a wetland.
11. A developer wants to extend a golf course into a wetland. Outline environmental arguments you could make against this plan.

STANDARD 4, OBJECTIVE 3: ANALYZE THE PHYSICAL, CHEMICAL, AND BIOLOGICAL DYNAMICS OF THE OCEANS AND THE FLOW OF ENERGY THROUGH THE OCEANS.

Lesson Objectives

- Describe how the oceans formed.
- State how the oceans influence Earth.
- Describe the makeup of ocean water.
- Identify ocean zones.

Introduction

Much of Earth's surface is covered with oceans. That's why Earth is called the "water planet." Without all that water, Earth would be a very different place. The oceans affect Earth's atmosphere. They also influence its climate. They are home to many living things as well. You might think that oceans have always covered Earth's surface. But you would be wrong!

How the Oceans Formed

When Earth formed 4.6 billion years ago, it would not have been called the "water planet." There were no oceans then. In fact, there was no liquid water at all. Early Earth was too hot for liquid water to form. It consisted only of molten rock.

Water on Early Earth

Over time, Earth cooled. The surface hardened to become solid rock. But volcanic eruptions, like the one in image right, kept bringing magma and gases to the surface through a process called outgassing. One of the gases was water vapor. More water vapor came from asteroids and comets that crashed into Earth. As Earth cooled still more, the water vapor condensed. This was Earth's first liquid water. At last, the oceans could start to form.

Volcanoes were one source of water vapor on ancient Earth. What were other sources?

Ancient Oceans

Earth's crust consists of many tectonic plates. The plates move over time. That's why the continents have changed their shapes and positions during Earth's history. As the continents changed, so did the oceans. About 250 million years ago, there was one huge land mass. With a single land mass, Earth's waters formed a vast ocean. This ocean has been called Panthalassa. You can see it in the image below:

Earth's Oceans 250 Million Years Ago

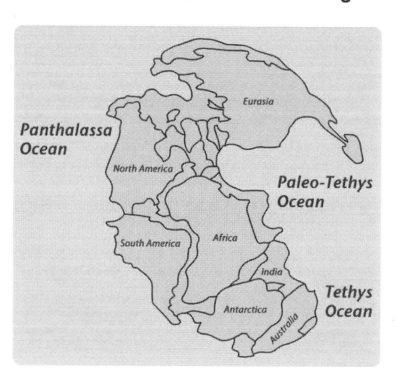

By 180 million years ago, the huge land mass began to break up. The continents started to drift apart. Slowly, the continents moved to where they are today. The oceans changed as well. Panthalassa broke into smaller oceans. Over time, it formed the Pacific, Atlantic, Indian, and Arctic Oceans. Even today, the waters of all the oceans are connected. That's why some people refer to the oceans together as the "World Ocean."

THE OCEANS' INFLUENCE

Oceans cover more than 70 percent of Earth's surface. They make up 97 percent of its surface water. It's no surprise that they have a big influence on the planet. They affect the atmosphere, climate, and living things.

Oceans and the Atmosphere

Oceans are the major source of water vapor in the atmosphere. Sunlight heats water near the surface, as shown in the diagram below. As the water warms, some of it evaporates. The water vapor rises into the air. It may form clouds and precipitation. Precipitation provides the freshwater needed by plants and other living things.

Gas Exchange Between Oceans and Atmosphere

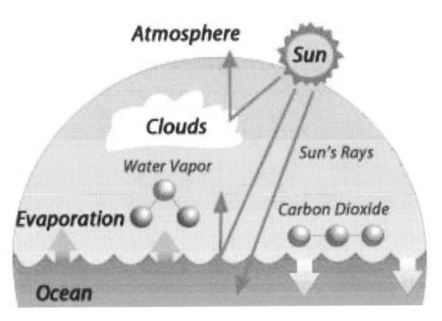

The oceans and atmosphere exchange gases. Why does water vapor enter the atmosphere from the water?

Ocean water also absorbs gases from the air. It absorbs oxygen and carbon dioxide. Oxygen is needed by living things in the oceans. Much of the dissolved carbon dioxide sinks to the bottom of the water. Carbon dioxide is a major cause of global warming. By absorbing carbon dioxide, the oceans help control global warming.

Oceans And Climate

Compared with inland areas, coastal areas have a milder climate. They are warmer in the winter and cooler in the summer. That's because land near an ocean is influenced by the temperature of the water. The temperature of ocean water is moderate and stable. Why? There are two major reasons:

- Ocean water is much slower to warm up and cool down than land. As a result, it never gets as hot or cold as land.
- Water flows through all the world's oceans. Therefore, warm water from the equator mixes with cold water from the poles. The warm and cold water tend to "cancel each other out."

Even inland temperatures are milder because of oceans. Without oceans, there would be much bigger temperature swings all over Earth and life would not be able to exist as it does now.

Oceans and Living Things

The oceans also provide a home to many living things. In fact, a greater number of organisms live in the oceans than on land. Coral reefs have more living things than almost anywhere else on Earth.

Why Is Ocean Water Salty?

Ocean water is salty because water dissolves minerals out of rocks. This happens whenever water flows over or through rocks. Much of this water ends up in the oceans. Minerals dissolved in water form salts. Mineral salts become more concentrated in ocean water. That's because a lot of the water evaporates. When it does, it leaves the salts behind. As a result, ocean water is much saltier than other water on Earth.

How Salty Is Ocean Water?

Did you ever go swimming in the ocean? If you did, then you probably tasted the salts in the water. By mass, salts make up about 3.5 percent of ocean water.

The Figure below shows the most common minerals in ocean water. The main minerals are sodium and chloride. They form the salt known as sodium chloride. You may know it as table salt.

What percentage of the salts in ocean water is sodium chloride?

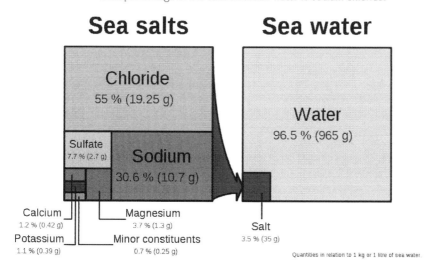

The amount of salts in ocean water varies from place to place. For example, near the mouth of a river, ocean water may be less salty. That's because river water contains less salt than ocean water. Where the ocean is warm, the water may be more salty. Can you explain why? (Hint: More water evaporates when the water is warm.)

Ocean Zones

In addition to the amount of salts, other conditions in ocean water vary from place to place. They include the amount of nutrients in the water and how much sunlight the water gets. These conditions depend mainly on two factors: distance from shore and depth of water. Oceans are divided into zones based on these two factors. The ocean floor makes up another zone. The diagram below describes all these zones.

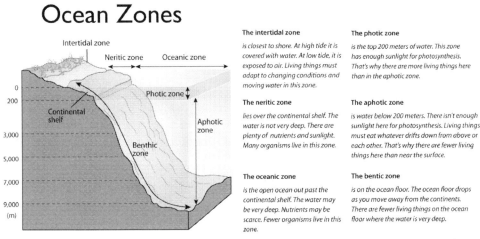

Ocean Zones

The intertidal zone

is closest to shore. At high tide it is covered with water. At low tide, it is exposed to air. Living things must adapt to changing conditions and moving water in this zone.

The neritic zone

lies over the continental shelf. The water is not very deep. There are plenty of nutrients and sunlight. Many organisms live in this zone.

The oceanic zone

is the open ocean out past the continental shelf. The water may be very deep. Nutrients may be scarce. Fewer organisms live in this zone.

The photic zone

is the top 200 meters of water. This zone has enough sunlight for photosynthesis. That's why there are more living things here than in the aphotic zone.

The aphotic zone

is water below 200 meters. There isn't enough sunlight here for photosynthesis. Living things must eat whatever drifts down from above or each other. That's why there are fewer living things here than near the surface.

The bentic zone

is on the ocean floor. The ocean floor drops as you move away from the continents. There are fewer living things on the ocean floor where the water is very deep.

Distance from shore defines some ocean zones. Depth of water defines others. Which zone is on the ocean floor?

Zones Based On Distance From Shore

There are three main ocean zones based on distance from shore. They are the intertidal zone, neritic zone, and oceanic zone. Distance from shore influences how many nutrients are in the water. Why? Most nutrients are washed into ocean water from land. Therefore, water closer to shore tends to have more nutrients. Living things need nutrients. So distance from shore also influences how many organisms live in the water.

Zones Based On Depth Of Water

Two main zones based on depth of water are the photic zone and aphotic zone.
The photic zone is the top 200 meters of water. The aphotic zone is water deeper than 200
meters. The deeper you go, the darker the water gets. That's because sunlight cannot
penetrate very far under water. Sunlight is needed for photosynthesis. Therefore, depth of
water determines whether photosynthesis is possible. There is enough sunlight for
photosynthesis only in the photic zone. Water also gets colder as you go deeper. The
weight of the water pressing down from above increases as well. At great depths, life
becomes very difficult. The pressure is so high that it can crush most living things.

Water Pressure and Depth

Pressure is the amount of force acting on a given area. As you go deeper in the ocean, the
pressure exerted by the water increases steadily. That's because there is more and more
water pressing down on you from above. shows how pressure changes with depth. For
each additional meter below the surface, pressure increases by 10 kPa. At 30 meters below
the surface, the pressure is double the pressure at the surface. At a depth greater than 500
meters, the pressure is too great for humans to withstand without special equipment to
protect them. At nearly 11,000 meters below the surface, the pressure is tremendous.

LESSON SUMMARY

- Early Earth was too hot for liquid water to form. Eventually Earth cooled. Water vapor from volcanoes and objects in space condensed. Oceans finally formed. The oceans changed size and shape as continents drifted.
- Oceans have a big influence on Earth. They exchange gases with the atmosphere. They prevent very hot and very cold temperatures. They are home to many living things.
- Dissolved mineral salts wash into the ocean. As ocean water evaporates, it leaves the salts behind. This makes the water saltier. Ocean water is about 3.5 percent salts. The main salt is sodium chloride.
- The ocean is divided into many zones. Some are based on distance from shore. Some are based on depth of water. The ocean floor is another zone.

Lesson Review Questions
1. State why there was no liquid water on ancient Earth.
2. Describe 2 ways the oceans influences Earth's atmosphere.
3. Describe how ocean water properties change as you go deeper in the water.
4. Define the intertidal zone, how do the conditions in this zone affect living things?
5. Compare and contrast the photic and aphotic zones.
6. Describe how water pressure in the ocean changes as depth increases.

OCEANIC MOVEMENTS

Lesson Objectives

- Describe how waves move through water.
- Explain what causes tides.
- Give an overview of surface currents.
- Identify the cause of deep currents.
- Describe upwelling.

Waves

Most ocean waves are caused by winds. A wave is the transfer of energy through matter. Ocean waves transfer energy from wind through water. The energy of a wave may travel for thousands of miles. However, the water itself moves very little. The Figure below shows how water molecules move when a wave goes by.

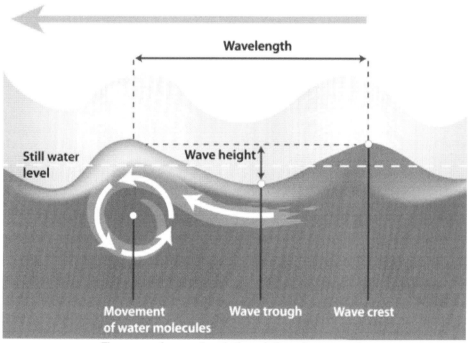

The energy of a wave travels through the water as a medium.

THE SIZE OF WAVES

The diagram above also shows how the size of waves is measured. The highest point of a wave is the crest. The lowest point is the trough. The vertical distance between a crest and a trough is the height of the wave. Wave height is also called amplitude. The horizontal distance between two crests is the wavelength. Both amplitude and wavelength are measures of wave size. The size of a wave depends on how fast, how far, and how long the wind blows. The greater each of these factors is, the bigger a wave will be. Some of the biggest waves occur with hurricanes. A hurricane is a storm that forms over the ocean. Its winds may blow more than 150 miles per hour! The winds also travel over long distances and may last for many days.

Breaking Waves

In shallow water, the waves touch the bottom. Dragging on the bottom causes the waves to slow down. They start to pile up. They get steeper and tip forward. When they reach the shore, the waves topple over and break.

Tsunamis

Not all waves are caused by winds. Earthquakes also send waves through water. A tsunami is a wave caused by an earthquake. It may be a very big wave. When a tsunami reaches shallow water near shore, it is likely to flood the land. Tsunamis often cause deaths and destroy property.

Tides

Tides are daily changes in the level of ocean water. They occur all around the globe. High tides occur when the water reaches its highest level. Low tides occur when the water reaches its lowest level. Tides keep cycling from high to low and back again. The water level rises and falls twice a day. As a result, in most places there are two high tides and two low tides every 24 hours. In the figure below, you can see the difference between high and low tides. The difference between the high and low tide is the tidal range.

Bay of Fundy Tides

High Tide

Low Tide

Where is the intertidal zone in this picture?

Why Tides Occur

The Figure below shows why tides occur. The main reason is the pull of the moon's gravity on Earth and its oceans. The pull is greatest on whatever is closest to the moon. As a result:

- Water on the side of Earth facing the moon is pulled hardest by the moon's gravity. This causes a bulge of water on that side of Earth. This creates a high tide.
- Earth itself is pulled harder by the moon's gravity than is the ocean on the side of Earth opposite the moon. As a result, there is bulge of water on that side of Earth as well. This creates another high tide.
- With water bulging on two sides of Earth, there's less water left on the rest of Earth. This creates low tides on the other sides.

Spring Tides and Neap Tides

The sun's gravity also pulls on Earth and its oceans. However, even though the sun is much larger than the moon, the pull of the sun's gravity isn't as great. That's because the sun is much farther away. The sun just strengthens or weakens the moon's influence on tides. The Figure below shows the position of the moon relative to the sun at different times during the month. This position determines how the sun affects tides. It creates either spring tides or neap tides.

High and low tides are due mainly to the pull of the moon.

Spring tides occur during the new moon and full moon. The sun and moon are in a straight line. Their gravity combines to cause very high and very low tides. These tides have the greatest difference between high and low tides.

Neap tides occur during the first and third quarters of the moon. The moon and sun are at right angles to each other. Their gravity pulls on the oceans in different directions. These tides have the least difference between high and low tides.

The sun and moon both affect Earth

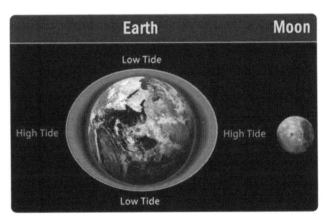

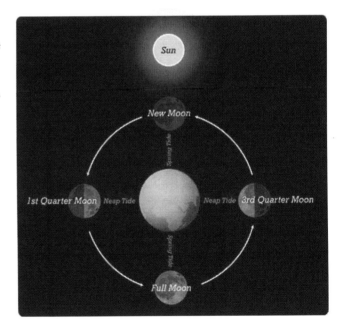

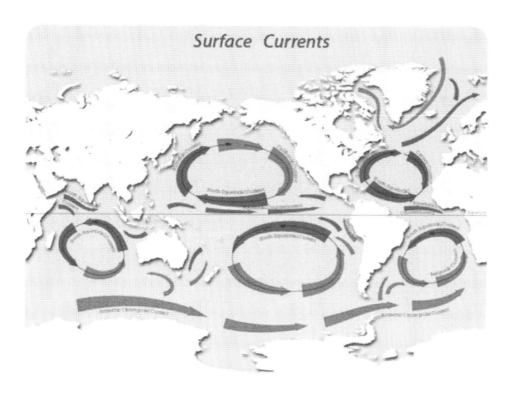

Surface Currents

Surface Currents

Another way ocean water moves is in currents. A current is a stream of moving water that flows through the ocean. Surface currents are caused mainly by winds. Major surface currents are shown in The Figure below. They flow in a clockwise direction in the Northern Hemisphere. In the Southern Hemisphere, they flow in the opposite direction.

Coriolis Effect

The Coriolis effect describes how Earth's rotation steers winds and surface ocean currents. Coriolis causes freely moving objects to appear to move to the right in the Northern Hemisphere and to the left in the Southern Hemisphere. The objects themselves are actually moving straight, but the Earth is rotating beneath them, so they seem to bend or curve. That's why it is incorrect to call Coriolis a force. It is not forcing anything to happen!

An example might make the Coriolis effect easier to visualize. If an airplane flies 500 miles due north, it will not arrive at the city that was due north of it when it began its journey. Over the time it takes for the airplane to fly 500 miles, that city moved, along with the Earth it sits on. The airplane will therefore arrive at a city to the west of the original city (in the Northern Hemisphere), unless the pilot has compensated for the change. So to reach his intended destination, the pilot must also veer right while flying north.

As wind or an ocean current moves, the Earth spins underneath it. As a result, an object moving north or south along the Earth will appear to move in a curve instead of in a straight line. Wind or water that travels toward the poles from the equator is deflected to the east, while wind or water that travels toward the equator from the poles gets bent to the west. The Coriolis effect bends the direction of surface currents to the right in the Northern Hemisphere and left in the Southern Hemisphere.

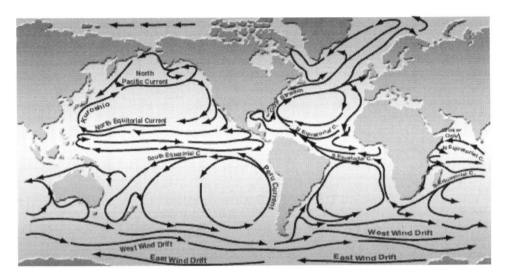

SURFACE CURRENTS AND CLIMATE

Large ocean currents can have a big impact on the climate of nearby coasts. The Gulf Stream, for example, carries warm water from the Gulf of Mexico up the eastern coast of North America and into Europe. This keep the temperatures in these regions more moderate.

Deep Currents

Currents also flow deep below the surface of the ocean. Deep currents are large convection currents. A convection current is a vertical current that flows because of differences in density at the top and bottom. Density is defined as the amount of mass per unit of volume. More dense water takes up less space than less dense water. It has the same mass but less volume. This makes denser water heavier and so it sinks. Less dense water rises. Rising and sinking water creates a convection current.

Water becomes more dense when it is colder and when it has higher concentration of salt. In the North Atlantic Ocean, cold winds chill the water at the surface. Sea ice forms from fresh water. This leaves behind a lot of salt in the seawater. This cold, dense water sinks to the bottom of the North Atlantic. Downwelling can take place in other places where surface water becomes very dense (see Figure below).

Deep currents flow because of differences in density of ocean water.

Upwelling
Sometimes deep ocean water rises to the surface. This is called upwelling. This figure shows why it happens. Strong winds blow surface water away from shore. This allows deeper water to flow to the surface and take its place.

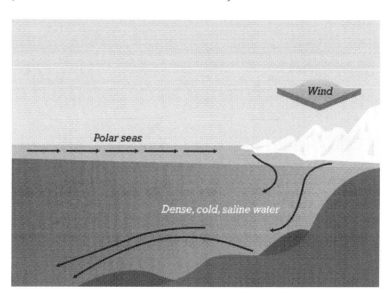

Polar seas

Wind

Dense, cold, saline water

Upwelling

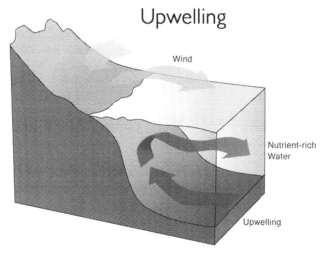

Wind

Nutrient-rich Water

Upwelling

An upwelling occurs when deep ocean water rises to the surface.

When water comes up from the deep, it brings a lot of nutrients with it. That's because nutrients settle to the bottom over time. The nutrients brought to the surface support many living things.

LESSON SUMMARY

- Most ocean waves are caused by winds. The size of a wave depends on how fast, how far, and how long the wind blows. Tsunamis are waves caused by earthquakes.
- Tides are daily changes in the level of ocean water. They are caused mainly by the pull of the moon's gravity on Earth and its oceans. The sun's gravity also influences tides.
- Surface currents are like streams flowing through the surface of the ocean. They are caused mainly by winds. Earth's rotation influences their direction. This is called the Coriolis effect. Surface currents may affect the climate of nearby coasts.
- Deep currents are convection currents that occur far below the surface. They are caused by differences in density of ocean water.
- Upwelling occurs when deep ocean water rises to the surface. It brings nutrients with it. The nutrients support many organisms.

LESSON REVIEW QUESTIONS

1. Identify two causes of ocean waves.
2. What is the Coriolis effect?
3. Define density. How is the density of water related to its temperature?
4. Describe upwelling. State why it occurs.
5. Explain how the moon and sun cause Earth's tides.
6. Compare and contrast surface currents and deep currents.
7. Compare and contrast El Niño and La Niña.

Points to Consider

- Upwelling brings nutrients to the surface from the ocean floor. Nutrients are important resources for ocean life. However, they aren't the only resources on the ocean floor.
- What other resources do you think might be found on the ocean floor?
- It's hard to get resources from the ocean floor. Can you explain why?

Going Further

This animation shows the effect of the Moon and Sun on the tides:
http://www.onr.navy.mil/focus/ocean/motion/tides1.htm.

CHAPTER REVIEW

1. Why were there no oceans on early Earth?
2. Where did the water come from that formed the oceans?
3. What is salinity?
4. Where did the salinity of oceans come from?
5. What is pressure?
6. What causes changes in pressure in the ocean?
7. What is temperature?
8. What causes changes in temperature in the ocean?
9. What causes waves?
10. What causes tides?
11. Compare and contrast spring tides and neap tides.
12. Describe how the ocean changes with depth.
13. What are the four ocean life zones, and what are the conditions like in each?
14. What is the intertidal zone, and what are the conditions there?
15. Describe how sonar works.
16. Sketch and label the features of the ocean floor.
17. What causes the global wind belts?
18. Sketch and label the global wind belts.
19. What is the Coriolis Effect?
20. How are the Global Wind Belts related to ocean currents?
21. Compare and contrast warm and cold water ocean currents.
22. Describe how ocean currents affect local climates.
23. Compare and contrast local (regional) sea level changes and world-wide (eustatic) sea level changes.
24. What is upwelling, and how does it occur?

PEOPLE + PLANET

CHAPTER 5

STANDARD 5: STUDENTS WILL UNDERSTAND HOW EARTH SCIENCE INTERACTS WITH SOCIETY

Objective 1: Characterize Earth as a changing and complex system of interacting spheres.

The Earth is made up of 4 main spheres: the biosphere (all living/once living things on Earth) the geosphere (all the rocks on Earth) the atmosphere (all the air on the Earth) and the hydrosphere (all the water on the Earth). These spheres interact with each other as energy and matter cycle through them. These interactions give rise to the processes that shape our Earth.

Earth's systems (all the things that make the earth work) are dynamic and continually react to natural and human-caused changes. In the following sections you will see examples of this in both the natural world and humans' influence on Earth.

TECHNOLOGICAL ADVANCES INCREASE HUMAN KNOWLEDGE

Satellites
One of the first uses of rockets in space was to launch satellites. A satellite is an object that orbits a larger object. An orbit is a circular or elliptical path around an object. The Moon was Earth's first satellite, but now many human-made "artificial satellites" orbit the planet. Thousands of artificial satellites have been put into orbit around Earth. We have even put satellites into orbit around the Moon, the Sun, Venus, Mars, Jupiter, and Saturn.

There are four main types of satellites:

Satellites operate with solar panels for energy.

- Imaging satellites take pictures of Earth's surface for military or scientific purposes. Imaging satellites study the Moon and other planets.
- Communications satellites receive and send signals for telephone, television, or other types of communications.
- Navigational satellites are used for navigation systems, such as the Global Positioning System (GPS).
- The International Space Station, the largest artificial satellite, is designed for humans to live in space while conducting scientific research.

Can you forecast your health?

You can use a thermometer to better understand your health just like a meteorologist uses one to better understand the weather. A thermometer will help you forecast your health just as it will help to forecast the weather. Other tools, like barometers, also help with weather forecasting.

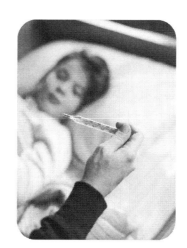

COLLECTING WEATHER DATA

To make a weather forecast, the conditions of the atmosphere must be known for that location and for the surrounding area. Temperature, air pressure, and other characteristics of the atmosphere must be measured and the data collected.

THERMOMETER

Thermometers measure temperature. In an old-style mercury thermometer, mercury is placed in a long, very narrow tube with a bulb. Because mercury is temperature sensitive, it expands when temperatures are high and contracts when they are low. A scale on the outside of the thermometer matches up with the air temperature.

Some modern thermometers use a coiled strip composed of two kinds of metal, each of which conducts heat differently. As the temperature rises and falls, the coil unfolds or curls up tighter. Other modern thermometers measure infrared radiation or electrical resistance. Modern thermometers usually produce digital data that can be fed directly into a computer.

BAROMETER

Meteorologists use barometers to measure air pressure. A barometer may contain water, air, or mercury, but like thermometers, barometers are now mostly digital.

A change in barometric pressure indicates that a change in weather is coming. If air pressure rises, a high pressure cell is on the way and clear skies can be expected. If pressure falls, a low pressure cell is coming and will likely bring storm clouds. Barometric pressure data over a larger area can be used to identify pressure systems, fronts, and other weather systems.

WEATHER STATIONS

Weather stations contain some type of thermometer and barometer. Other instruments measure different characteristics of the atmosphere, such as wind speed, wind direction, humidity, and amount of precipitation. These instruments are placed in various locations so that they can check the atmospheric characteristics of that location (Figure below). Weather stations are located on land, the surface of the sea, and in orbit all around the world.

According to the World Meteorological Organization, weather information is collected from 15 satellites, 100 stationary buoys, 600 drifting buoys, 3,000 aircraft, 7,300 ships, and some 10,000 land-based stations.

RADIOSONDES

Radiosondes measure atmospheric characteristics, such as temperature, pressure, and humidity as they move through the air. Radiosondes in flight can be tracked to obtain wind speed and direction. Radiosondes use a radio to communicate the data they collect to a computer. Radiosondes are launched from about 800 sites around the globe twice daily to provide a profile of the atmosphere. Radiosondes can be dropped from a balloon or airplane to make measurements as they fall. This is done to monitor storms, for example, since they are dangerous places for airplanes to fly.

A land-based weather station.

RADAR

Radar stands for Radio Detection and Ranging (Figure below). A transmitter sends out radio waves that bounce off the nearest object and then return to a receiver. Weather radar can sense many characteristics of precipitation: its location, motion, intensity, and the likelihood of future precipitation. Doppler radar can also track how fast the precipitation falls. Radar can outline the structure of a storm and can be used to estimate its possible effects.

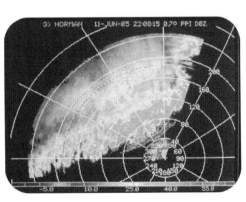

Radar view of a line of thunderstorms.

SATELLITES

Weather satellites have been increasingly important sources of weather data since the first one was launched in 1952. Weather satellites are the best way to monitor large-scale systems, such as storms. Satellites are able to record long-term changes, such as the amount of ice cover over the Arctic Ocean in September each year.

Weather satellites may observe all energy from all wavelengths in the electromagnetic spectrum. Visible light images record storms, clouds, fires, and smog. Infrared images record clouds, water and land temperatures, and features of the ocean, such as ocean currents (Figure below).

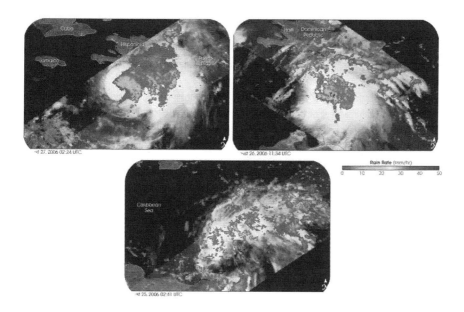

Infrared data superimposed on a satellite image shows rainfall patterns in Hurricane Ernesto in 2006.

An online guide to weather forecasting from the University of Illinois is found here: http://ww2010.atmos.uiuc.edu/%28Gh%29/guides/mtr/fcst/home.rxml.

SUMMARY

Various instruments measure weather conditions: thermometers measure air temperature, and barometers measure air pressure. Satellites monitor weather and also help with understanding long-term changes in climate. Radar is used to monitor precipitation.

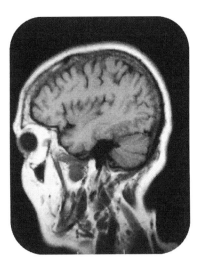

How is a seismologist like a medical doctor?

Just as a medical doctor uses an MRI, CT scan, or x-ray to see inside a patient's body, seismologists use wave energy to learn about Earth's interior. The difference is that the doctor can run the energy through the patient at any time. Scientists need to wait for an earthquake to get information about Earth's interior

With these and other technologies we are able to gain more knowledge about the Earth around us and in turn are better able to predict when physical changes will occur here on our planet. With these predictions we can save lives and keep our future safe. *source: written by compiler of all of this information.*

1. **Design and conduct an experiment that investigates how Earth's biosphere, geosphere, atmosphere, or hydrosphere reacts to human-caused change.**

Try this: think of an experiment where you can investigate how Earth's biosphere, geosphere, atmosphere, or hydrosphere reacts to human-caused change. Keep track of your data in your science journal and share what you learn with a friend. (source: written by compiler of this info)

2. **Research and report on how scientists study feedback loops to inform the public about Earth's interacting systems.**

Once you have seen patterns in what you observed in the above mentioned "try this" take another look at your conclusion. Does it give you any hint as to why you saw what you did? Is there any way to mitigate (take care of) what you observed? Is there something we as humans can do to make the results of the human-caused change not so severe? As you go through this process you are going through the process known as "feedback loops." You are able to see the results of some action and by that information you come up with another way to approach the issue you are investigating. Welcome to the process of science! Scientists use these feedback loops to inform the public about Earth's interacting systems.

STANDARD 5, OBJECTIVE 2: DESCRIBE HOW HUMANS DEPEND ON EARTH'S RESOURCES.

Earth's resources are distributed

For information about Utah's own resources are distributed check out this website: http://naturalresources.utah.gov/about-dnr.html

Will water cause the next war?

Wars have been fought over oil, but many people predict that the next war will be fought over water. Certainly, water is becoming scarcer.

Water Distribution

Water is unevenly distributed around the world. Large portions of the world, such as much of northern Africa, receive very little water relative to their population (Figure below). The map shows the relationship between water supply and population by river basin.

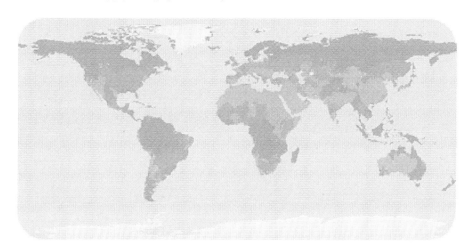

Blue means there is a lot of river water for each person who lives in the river basin.
Salmon pink means there is very little river water for each person who lives in the river basin.

Over time, there will be less water per person within many river basins as the population grows and global temperatures increase so that some water sources are lost. In 2025, many nations, even developed nations, are projected to have less water per person than now (Figure below).

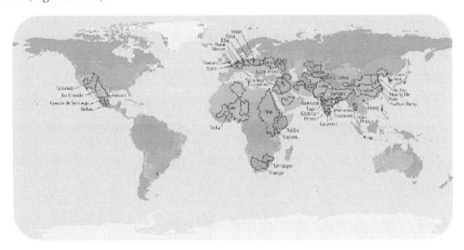

The same map but projected into 2025.

Water Shortages

Water scarcity is a problem now and will become an even larger problem in the future as water sources are reduced or polluted and population grows. In 1995, about 40% of the world's population faced water scarcity (Figure below). Scientists estimate that by the year 2025, nearly half of the world's people won't have enough water to meet their daily needs. Nearly one-quarter of the world's people will have less than 500 m3 of water to use in an entire year. That amount is less water in a year than some people in the United States use in one day.

Nearly Half the World Will Live With Water Scarcity by 2025

Figure 2: Global Renewable Water Supply per Person, 1995 and 2025 (projected)

Water Supply (m3/person /year)	1995 Population (millions)	1995 Percent of Total	2025 Population (millions)	2025 Percent of Total
<500	1,077	19.0	1,783	24.5
500-1,000	587	10.4	624	8.6
1,000-1,700	669	11.8	1,077	14.8
Subtotal	2,333	41.2	3,484	47.9
>1,700	3,091	54.6	3,494	48.0
Unallocated	241	4.2	296	4.0
Total	5,665	100.0	7,274	100.0

Source: WRI. The 2025 estimates are considered conservative because they are based on the United Nations' low-range projections for population growth, which has population peaking at 7.3 billion in 2025 (UNDP 1999:3). In addition, a slight mismatch between the water runoff and population data sets leaves 4 percent of the global population unaccounted in this analysis.

Water supply compared to population.

DROUGHTS

Droughts occur when a region experiences unusually low precipitation for months or years (Figure right). Periods of drought may create or worsen water shortages.

Human activities can contribute to the frequency and duration of droughts. For example, deforestation keeps trees from returning water to the atmosphere by transpiration; part of the water cycle becomes broken. Because it is difficult to predict when droughts will happen, it is difficult for countries to predict how serious water shortages will be each year.

Extended periods with lower than normal rainfall cause droughts.

EFFECT OF CHANGING CLIMATE

Global warming will change patterns of rainfall and water distribution. As the Earth warms, regions that currently receive an adequate supply of rain may shift. Regions that rely on snowmelt may find that there is less snow and the melt comes earlier and faster in the spring, causing the water to run off and not be available through the dry summers. A change in temperature and precipitation would completely change the types of plants and animals that can live successfully in that region.

WATER SCARCITY

Water scarcity can have dire consequences for the people, the economy, and the environment. Without adequate water, crops and livestock dwindle and people go hungry. Industry, construction, and economic development is halted, causing a nation to sink further into poverty. The risk of regional conflicts over scarce water resources rises. People die from diseases, thirst, or even in war over scarce resources.

California's population is growing by hundreds of thousands of people a year, but much of the state receives as much annual rainfall as Morocco. With fish populations crashing, global warming, and the demands of the country's largest agricultural industry, the pressures on our water supply are increasing. Find out more at: http://science.kqed.org/quest/video/state-of-thirst-californias-water-future/.

CONFLICTS OVER WATER

As water supplies become scarce, conflicts will arise between the individuals or nations that have enough clean water and those that do not (Figurebelow). Some of today's greatest tensions are happening in places where water is scarce. Water disputes may add to tensions between countries where differing national interests and withdrawal rights have been in conflict. Just as with energy resources today, wars may erupt over water.

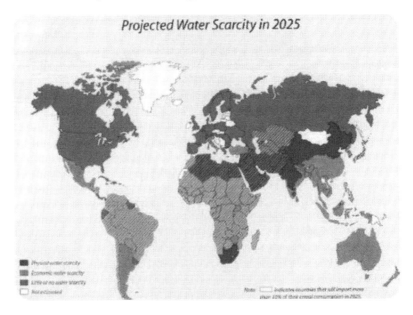

By 2025, many nations will face water scarcity. For the nations in red, there will simply not be enough fresh water; the nations in brown may not be able to afford to supply their citizens with fresh water.

Water disputes are happening along 260 different river systems that cross national boundaries. Some of these disputes are potentially very serious. International water laws, such as the Helsinki Rules, help interpret water rights among countries.

SUMMARY

- A lot of the problem with water is that it is not evenly distributed across the planet.
- Many of the world's people live with water scarcity, and that percentage will increase as populations increase and climate changes.
- Some people predict that, just as wars are fought over energy now, future wars will be fought over water.

Practice

Use this resource to answer the questions that follow:

http://www.youtube.com/watch?v=XGgYTcPzexE

1. What is water scarcity?
2. Why do people take water for granted?
3. How much freshwater is there on Earth?
4. How many people do not have access to clean water?
5. What will occur by 2025?
6. What is physical water scarcity? Where does this occur?
7. What is economic water scarcity? Where does this occur?

Review

8. How will changing climate affect the availability and distribution of water?
9. How do human activities affect the occurrence of droughts?
10. How do so many people live with so little water?

Could this land be used for agriculture?

Probably not. The quality of soil is very important in determining what can grow in a particular area. Good soil is not so easy to come by. Soil should be considered another resource that we, as a population, must strive to protect.

SOIL AND WATER RESOURCES

Theoretically, soil and water are renewable resources. However, they may be ruined by careless human actions.

SOIL

Soil is a mixture of eroded rock, minerals, partly decomposed organic matter, and other materials. It is essential for plant growth, so it is the foundation of terrestrial ecosystems. Soil is important for other reasons as well. For example, it removes toxins from water and breaks down wastes.

Although renewable, soil takes a very long time to form—up to hundreds of millions of years. So, for human purposes, soil is a nonrenewable resource. It is also constantly depleted of nutrients through careless use, and eroded by wind and water. For example, misuse of soil caused a huge amount of it to simply blow away in the 1930s during the Dust Bowl (see Figure opposite). Soil must be used wisely to preserve it for the future. Conservation practices include contour plowing and terracing. Both reduce soil erosion. Soil also must be protected from toxic wastes.

The Dust Bowl occurred between 1933 and 1939 in Oklahoma and other southwestern U.S. states. Plowing had exposed prairie soil. Drought turned the soil to dust. Intense dust storms blew away vast quantities of the soil. Much of the soil blew all the way to the Atlantic Ocean.

WATER

Water is essential for all life on Earth. For human use, water must be fresh. Of all the water on Earth, only 1 percent is fresh, liquid water. Most of the rest is either salt water in the ocean or ice in glaciers and ice caps.

Although water is constantly recycled through the water cycle, it is in danger. Over-use and pollution of freshwater threaten the limited supply that people depend on. Already, more than 1 billion people worldwide do not have adequate freshwater. With the rapidly growing human population, the water shortage is likely to get worse.

KQED: ARE WE IN DANGER OF RUNNING OUT OF WATER?

California's population is growing by 600,000 people a year, but much of the state receives as much annual rainfall as Morocco. With fish populations crashing, global warming, and the demands of the country's largest agricultural industry, the pressures on our water supply are increasing. Is the U.S.'s largest population in danger of running out of water?

For additional information see:
http://www.kqed.org/quest/television/state-of-thirst-californias-water-future

TOO MUCH OF A GOOD THING

Water pollution comes from many sources. One of the biggest sources is runoff. Runoff picks up chemicals such as fertilizer from agricultural fields, lawns, and golf courses. It carries the chemicals to bodies of water. The added nutrients from fertilizer often cause excessive growth of algae, creating algal blooms (see Figure right). The algae use up oxygen in the water so that other aquatic organisms cannot survive. This has occurred over large areas of the ocean, creating dead zones, where low oxygen levels have killed all ocean life. A very large dead zone exists in the Gulf of Mexico. Measures that can help prevent these problems include cutting down on fertilizer use. Preserving wetlands also helps because wetlands filter runoff water.

Algal Bloom. Nutrients from fertilizer in runoff caused this algal bloom.

SUMMARY

- Soil and water are renewable resources but may be ruined by careless human actions. Soil can be depleted of nutrients. It can also be eroded by wind or water.
- Over-use and pollution of freshwater threaten the limited supply that people depend on.

PRACTICE

Use this resources to answer the questions on Biogeochemical Cycles that follow.

http://www.hippocampus.org/Biology ⟶ Non-Majors Biology ⟶ Search:Human

1. What happens when fertilizer ends up in waterways?
2. Describe eutrophication.
3. What has happened at the mouth of the Mississippi River?

Will There Be Enough Fresh Water?
http://www.concord.org/activities/will-there-be-enough-fresh-water.

REVIEW

4. What is soil?
5. Why is soil considered a nonrenewable resource?
6. Why would you expect a dead zone to start near the mouth of a river, where the river flows into a body of water?

HOW RESOURCE DEVELOPMENT AND USE ALTERS EARTH SYSTEMS

How Will the Removal of the Elwha Dam Affect the Freshwater Ecosystem Upstream?

For over a hundred years in the Pacific Northwest, the Elwha freshwater ecosystem was being disturbed by the Elwha dam. Salmon that typically spawn upstream were not able to do so. Check it out: Restoring the Elwha:

http://www.ck12.org/rwa/Destroying-the-Dam/?eid=SCI.ESC.256.2&rtitle=Hydroelectric+Power&ref=%2Fconcept%2FDestroying-the-Dam

How were the salmon being affected by the dam? By simply removing the dam, will the ecosystem improve? What will change?

Extension Investigation

1. Hydoelectric power, a renewable energy source with no pollution, is an excellent alternative to fossil fuels. Removing the dam means removing a good source of power. How was the dam threatening the survival of salmon? Pacific Salmonids: Major Threats and Impacts Are there other threats to the survival of the salmon in the Pacific Northwest?
2. As mentioned in the video clip, scientists are paying close attention to the number of salmon present in the Upper Elwha River to assess how the ecosystem is improving. How are they measuring the population growth? If the salmon population increases in the ecosystem, how will that impact other organisms? Create a "before" food web and an "after" food web showing the other players that would be affected.
3. How will the shape of the river change as the dam is removed? How will incorporating log jams improve areas for salmon to spawn? Build a model or use a stream table to simulate the Elwha river with the dam and without the dam. Add log jams. Observe the velocity of stream flow and locations of sediment deposition.

Can we use up all of our sunlight?

No, we have a limitless supply of sunlight. That makes it a renewable resource. Products derived from fossil fuels, like the gasoline we use to drive our cars, are not renewable resources. We will eventually run out of fossil fuels.

Renewable Resources and Alternative Energy Sources

A resource is renewable if it is remade by natural processes at the same rate that humans use it up. Sunlight and wind are renewable resources because they will not be used up (Figure below). The rising and falling of ocean tides is another example of a resource in unlimited supply. A sustainable resource is a resource that is used in a way that meets the needs of the present without keeping future generations from meeting their needs. People can sustainably harvest wood, cork, and bamboo. Farmers can also grow crops sustainably by not planting the same crop in their soil year after year. Planting the same crop each year can remove nutrients from the soil. This means that wood, cork, bamboo, and crops can be sustainable resources.

Wind power, a renewable resource, shown here in a modern wind energy farm.

Alternative Energy Sources

A nonrenewable resource is one that cannot be replaced as easily as it is consumed. Fossil fuels are an example of nonrenewable resources. They take millions of years to form naturally, and so they cannot be replaced as fast as they are consumed. To take the place of fossil fuel use, alternative energy resources are being developed. These alternative energy sources often utilize renewable resources. The following are examples of sustainable alternative energy resources:

An example of solar power, using solar cells to convert sunlight into electricity.

- Solar power, which uses solar cells to turn sunlight into electricity (Figure above). The electricity can be used to power anything that uses normal coal-generated electricity.

- Wind power, which uses windmills to transform wind energy into electricity. It is used for less than 1% of the world's energy needs. But wind energy is growing fast. Every year, 30% more wind energy is used to create electricity.
- Hydropower (Figure below), which uses the energy of moving water to turn turbines (similar to windmills) or water wheels, that create electricity. This form of energy produces no waste or pollution. It is a renewable resource.

Hydropower plant.

- Geothermal power, which uses the natural flow of heat from the earth's core to produce steam. This steam is used to turn turbines which create electricity.
- Biomass is the mass of biological organisms. It is usually used to describe the amount of organic matter in a trophic level of an ecosystem. Biomass production involves using organic matter ("biomass") from plants to create electricity. Using corn to make ethanol fuel is an example of biomass generated energy. Biomass is generally renewable.
- Tides in the ocean can also turn a turbine to create electricity. This energy can then be stored until needed (Figure below).

Dam of the tidal power plant in the Rance River, Bretagne, France

GLOSSARY

biomass: Total mass of organisms at a trophic level.

biomass production: Use of organic matter (biomass) from plants to create electricity.

geothermal power: Electricity derived from the natural flow of heat from the earth's core.

hydropower: Electricity derived from the energy of moving water.

nonrenewable resource: Natural resource that is used up faster than it can be made by nature.

renewable resource: Natural resource that can be replaced as quickly as it is used.

sustainable resource: Resources that is used in a way that meets the needs of the present without keeping future generations from meeting their needs.

solar power: Electricity derived from the sun.

wind power: Electricity derived from the wind.

SUMMARY

Renewable resources can be replaced by natural processes as quickly as they are used. Alternative energy sources include wind power, solar power, hydropower, and geothermal power.

Practice

Use the resource below to answer the questions that follow:
http://www.youtube.com/watch?v=1cysa0nlv_E (3:54)

1. How much of the energy needs of the European Union in 2005 was supplied from renewable resources?
2. What energy producing techniques can be used to produce electricity? What techniques can be used to produce heat?
3. Why is biomass based energy known as the "Sleeping Giant"? What energy could it replace that some of the other techniques (such as tidal power) would have difficulty replacing?
4. What is Biogas? How is it produced? What resources is it targeted to replace?
5. Review
6. What does sustainable mean?
7. What are some ways that renewable resources can be used to generate energy?

SCIENTISTS PROVIDE DATA THAT INFORMS THE DISCUSSION OF EARTH RESOURCE USE

What is electronic waste? We obtain resources of developing nations. We also dump waste on these nations. Many of our electronic wastes, which we think are being recycled, end up in developing countries. These are known as electronic waste or e-waste. People pick through the wastes looking for valuable materials that they can sell, but this exposes them to many toxic compounds that are hazardous to them and the environment.

RESOURCE AVAILABILITY

SUPPLY

From the table in the previous lesson you can see that many of the resources we depend on are nonrenewable. Nonrenewable resources vary in their availability; some are very abundant and others are rare. Materials, such as gravel or sand, are technically nonrenewable, but they are so abundant that running out is no issue. Some resources are truly limited in quantity: when they are gone, they are gone, and something must be found that will replace them. There are even resources, such as diamonds and rubies, that are valuable in part because they are so rare.

PRICE

Besides abundance, a resource's value is determined by how easy it is to locate and extract. If a resource is difficult to use, it will not be used until the price for that resource becomes so great that it is worth paying for. For example, the oceans are filled with an abundant supply of water, but desalination is costly, so it is used only where water is really limited (Figurebelow). As the cost of desalination plants comes down, more will likely be built.

Tampa Bay, Florida, has one of the few desalination plants in the United States.

POLITICS

Politics is also part of determining resource availability and cost. Nations that have a desired resource in abundance will often export that resource to other countries, while countries that need that resource must import it from one of the countries that produces it. This situation is a potential source of economic and political trouble.

Of course the greatest example of this is oil. 11 countries have nearly 80% of all of the world's oil (Figure below). However, the biggest users of oil, the United States, China, and Japan, are all located outside this oil-rich region. This leads to a situation in which the availability and price of the oil is determined largely by one set of countries that have their own interests to look out for. The result has sometimes been war, which may have been attributed to all sorts of reasons, but at the bottom, the reason is oil.

The nations in green are the 11 biggest producers of oil; they are Algeria, Indonesia, Iran, Iraq, Kuwait, Libya, Nigeria, Qatar, Saudi Arabia, the United Arab Emirates, and Venezuela.

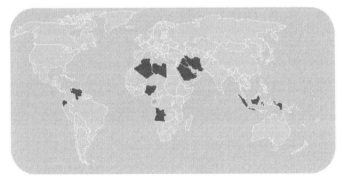

Waste

The topic of overconsumption was touched on in Concept Life on Earth. Many people in developed countries, such as the United States and most of Europe, use many more natural resources than people in many other countries. We have many luxury and recreational items, and it is often cheaper for us to throw something away than to fix it or just hang on to it for a while longer. This consumerism leads to greater resource use, but it also leads to more waste. Pollution from discarded materials degrades the land, air, and water (Figure below).

Pollution from discarded materials degrades the environment and reduces the availability of natural resources.

Natural resource use is generally lower in developing countries because people cannot afford many products. Some of these nations export natural resources to the developed world since their deposits may be richer and the cost of labor lower. Environmental regulations are often more lax, further lowering the cost of resource extraction.

SUMMARY

- The availability of a resource depends on how much of it there is and how hard it is to extract, refine, and transport to where it is needed.
- Politics plays an important role in resource availability since an unfavorable political situation can make a resource unavailable to a nation.
- Increased resource use generally means more waste; electronic waste from developed nations is a growing problem in the developing world.

Practice

Use this resource to answer the questions that follow.

http://www.youtube.com/watch?v=OJZey9GJQPO

1. Why are they melting computer circuit boards?
2. What toxic gases are given off?
3. What metals are they extracting from these computers?
4. What do CRTs contain?
5. What do computer batteries contain?
6. How can these chemicals harm people?
7. How much does recycling a computer cost in India?
8. What companies have committed to reducing the toxic chemicals in their products?

Review

9. Why does electronic waste that is generated in developed nations get dumped in developing nations?
10. Why is politics important in the availability of resources?
11. Why do some nations consume more goods and generate more waste than others?

Earth science literacy helps the public make informed choices

Knowledge is power. We have heard that phrase over and over as we are on this journey of gaining knowledge as we attend school. Knowledge about the Earth is key when we, as humans, choose how to use natural resources here on Earth. We are able to gain knowledge about where and when to use natural resources as we pay attention to Earth science literacy. These sources give us the knowledge we need to make informed choices about where to drill for oil, where the best wind plant locations would be, how to clean and conserve water, etc. (*source: written by compiler of information*)

STANDARD 5, OBJECTIVE 3: INDICATE HOW NATURAL HAZARDS POSE RISKS TO HUMANS.

Natural hazards

There is a great source from UGS - a PDF that contains a lot of great info specifically for Utah.

http://geology.utah.gov/online/pdf/pi-48.pdf

House damaged by the April 6, 2004 debris flow in Farmington, Utah.

Landslides: Events & Information

Landslides are common natural hazards in Utah. They often strike without warning and can be destructive and costly. Common types of landslides in Utah are debris flows, slides, and rock falls. Many landslides are associated with rising ground-water levels due to rainfall, snowmelt, and landscape irrigation.

Therefore, landslides in Utah typically move during the months of March, April, and May, although debris flows associated with intense thunderstorm rainfall are common in July.

Source for the above article:
http://geology.utah.gov/utahgeo/hazards/landslide/index.htm

PREVENT WILDFIRES: WHAT CAN YOU DO?

Debris Burning
- Check with your local officials to see if it is an "open burn season."
- Inquire with your local fire chief or fire warden to see if a permit is required.
- Have a shovel and water accessible and ready to go.
- Be prepared to stay near your burn until it is out and cold.
- Notify the city or county dispatch when you are ready to ignite.

Building Safe Campfires
- Clear campfire site down to bare soil.
- Circle pit with rocks.
- Build campfires away from overhanging branches, steep slopes, dry grass, and leaves.
- Keep a bucket of water and a shovel nearby.
- Never leave a campfire unattended.
- When putting out a campfire, drown the fire, stir it, and drown it again.
- Always have adult supervision.
- Be careful with gas lanterns, barbeque grills, gas stoves, and anything that can be a source of ignition for a wildfire.

Off-Road Safety
- Never park on or drive through dry grass.
- Grease trailer wheels, check tires, and ensure safety chains are not touching the ground.
- Internal combustion engines on off-road vehicles require a spark arrestor
- Check and clean the spark arrestor.
- Carry a shovel and fire extinguisher in your vehicle or OHV/ATV
- Spark from chainsaws, welding torches, and other equipment can cause wildfires.
- Please check local restrictions before using such equipment.

Fireworks Safety
Safety tips for the use of fireworks on PRIVATE LAND when authorized:
- Always read directions.
- Always have adult supervision
- Never use fireworks near dry grass or other flammable materials.
- Have a bucket of water and a hose nearby.
- Never attempt to re-light or "fix" fireworks.
- Fireworks are not toys.
- Use only Utah State Fire Marshal approved fireworks.

Source for above info:
http://www.utahfireinfo.gov/prevention/fire_safety.html

What causes the greatest damage in an earthquake?

This photo shows the Mission District of San Francisco burning after the 1906 earthquake. The greatest damage in earthquakes is usually not from the ground shaking. The greatest damage is caused by the effects of that shaking. In this earthquake, the shaking broke the gas mains and the water pipes. When the gas caught fire, there was no way to put it out. Fire causes the greatest damage in many earthquakes.

EARTHQUAKE!

An earthquake is sudden ground movement. This movement is caused by the sudden release of the energy stored in rocks. An earthquake happens when so much stress builds up in the rocks that the rocks break. An earthquake's energy is transmitted by seismic waves.

Causes of Earthquakes

Almost all earthquakes occur at plate boundaries. All types of plate boundaries have earthquakes. Convection within the Earth causes the plates to move. As the plates move, stresses build. When the stresses build too much, the rocks break. The break releases the energy that was stored in the rocks. The sudden release of energy is an earthquake. During an earthquake the rocks usually move several centimeters. Rarely, they may move as much as a few meters. Elastic rebound theory describes how earthquakes occur (see Figure next page).

Elastic rebound theory. Stresses build on both sides of a fault. The rocks deform plastically as seen in Time 2. When the stresses become too great, the rocks return to their original shape. To do this, the rocks move, as seen in Time 3. This movement releases energy, creating an earthquake.

Elastic rebound theory in an animation: http://earthquake.usgs.gov/learn/animations/animation.php?flash _title=Elastic+Rebound&flash_file=elasticrebound&flash_widt h=300&flash_height=350.

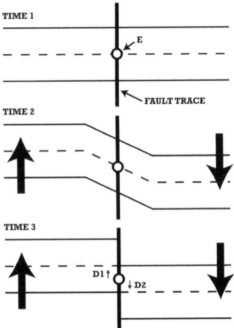

How can you prepare for an earthquake?

If you live in earthquake country the actions you take before, during, and after a quake could make the difference in your comfort for several days or even your survival.

Protecting Yourself in an Earthquake

There are many things you can do to protect yourself before, during, and after an earthquake.

BEFORE THE EARTHQUAKE

- Have an engineer evaluate the house for structural integrity. Make sure the separate pieces — floor, walls, roof, and foundation — are all well-attached to each other.
- Bracket or brace brick chimneys to the roof.
- Be sure that heavy objects are not stored in high places.
- Secure water heaters all around and at the top and bottom.
- Bolt heavy furniture onto walls with bolts, screws, or strap hinges.
- Replace halogen and incandescent light bulbs with fluorescent bulbs to lessen fire risk.
- Check to see that gas lines are made of flexible material so that they do not rupture. Any equipment that uses gas should be well secured.
- Everyone in the household should know how to shut off the gas line.
- Prepare an earthquake kit with three days supply of water and food, a radio, and batteries.
- Place flashlights all over the house and in the glove box of your car.

- Keep several fire extinguishers around the house to fight small fires.
- Be sure to have a first aid kit. Everyone should know basic first aid and CPR.
- Plan in advance how you will evacuate and where you will go. Do not plan on driving, as roadways will likely be damaged.

DURING THE EARTHQUAKE
- If you are in a building, get beneath a sturdy table, cover your head, and hold on.
- Stay away from windows, mirrors, and large furniture.
- If the building is structurally unsound, get outside as fast as possible.
- If you are outside, run to an open area away from buildings and power lines that may fall.
- If you are in a car, stay in the car and stay away from structures that might collapse, such as overpasses, bridges, or buildings.

AFTER THE EARTHQUAKE
- Be aware that aftershocks are likely.
- Avoid dangerous areas like hillsides that may experience a landslide.
- Turn off water and power to your home.
- Use your phone only if there is an emergency. Many people will be trying to get through to emergency services.
- Be prepared to wait for help or instructions. Assist others as necessary.

SUMMARY
- Before an earthquake, be sure that your home is secure and that you have supplies to last a few days.
- During an earthquake, get to a safe place.
- After an earthquake, avoid dangerous situations, wait for instructions, and assist as necessary.

FL**OO**DS

Why are there so many floods?

Floods are a natural part of the water cycle, but that doesn't make them any less terrifying. Put most simply, a flood is an overflow of water in one place. How can you prepare for a flood? What do you do if you're caught in one?

Causes of Floods

Floods usually occur when precipitation falls more quickly than water can be absorbed into the ground or carried away by rivers or streams. Waters may build up gradually over a period of weeks, when a long period of rainfall or snowmelt fills the ground with water and raises stream levels.

Extremely heavy rains across the Midwestern U.S. in April 2011 led to flooding of the rivers in the Mississippi River basin in May 2011 (Figures below and opposite).

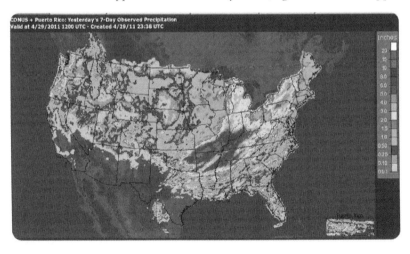

This map shows the accumulated rainfall across the U.S. in the days from April 22 to April 29, 2011.

April 14, 2010

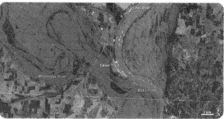

May 3, 2011

Record flow in the Ohio and Mississippi Rivers has to go somewhere. Normal spring river levels are shown in 2010. The flooded region in the image from May 3, 2011 is the New Madrid Floodway, where overflow water is meant to go. 2011 is the first time since 1927 that this floodway was used.

Flash Floods

Flash floods are sudden and unexpected, taking place when very intense rains fall over a very brief period (Figure below). A flash flood may do its damage miles from where the rain actually falls if the water travels far down a dry streambed.

A 2004 flash flood in England devastated two villages when 3-1/2 inches of rain fell in 60 minutes.

Buffers to Flooding

Heavily vegetated lands are less likely to experience flooding. Plants slow down water as it runs over the land, giving it time to enter the ground. Even if the ground is too wet to absorb more water, plants still slow the water's passage and increase the time between rainfall and the water's arrival in a stream; this could keep all the water falling over a region from hitting the stream at once. Wetlands act as a buffer between land and high water levels and play a key role in minimizing the impacts of floods. Flooding is often more severe in areas that have been recently logged.

Flood Protection

People try to protect areas that might flood with dams, and dams are usually very effective. But high water levels sometimes cause a dam to break and then flooding can be catastrophic. People may also line a river bank with levees, high walls that keep the stream within its banks during floods. A levee in one location may just force the high water up or downstream and cause flooding there. The New Madrid Overflow in the image above was created with the recognition that the Mississippi River sometimes simply cannot be contained by levees and must be allowed to flood.

Effects of Floods

Within the floodplain of the Nile, soils are fertile enough for productive agriculture. Beyond this, infertile desert soils prevent viable farming.

Not all the consequences of flooding are negative. Rivers deposit new nutrient-rich sediments when they flood, so floodplains have traditionally been good for farming. Flooding as a source of nutrients was important to Egyptians along the Nile River until the Aswan Dam was built in the 1960s. Although the dam protects crops and settlements from the annual floods, farmers must now use fertilizers to feed their cops.

Floods are also responsible for moving large amounts of sediments about within streams. These sediments provide habitats for animals, and the periodic movement of sediment is crucial to the lives of several types of organisms. Plants and fish along the Colorado River, for example, depend on seasonal flooding to rearrange sand bars.

"Floods 101" is a National Geographic video found in Environment Video, Natural Disasters, Landslides, and more:
http://video.nationalgeographic.com/video/player/environment/.

SUMMARY

- When the amount of water in a drainage exceeds the capacity of the drainage, there is a flood.
- Floods are made worse when vegetation is cleared, when the land is already soaked, or when hillsides have been logged.
- People build dams and levees to protect from flooding.
- Floods are a source of nutrients on a floodplain.

Practice

Use this resource to answer the questions that follow.

http://video.nationalgeographic.com/video/environment/environment-natural-disasters/landslides-and-more/floods/

1. Where are floods more likely to occur?
2. Why have farmers relied on floods?
3. What causes floods?
4. At what depth can a flood move a car? Why is this dangerous?
5. What cause the Mississippi Flood of 1993?
6. Why did Hurricane Katrina cause so much damage to New Orleans?
7. What could cause massive flooding today?

Review

1. How does a flash flood differ from another type of flood?
2. What was the role of flooding on the Nile River and what was the consequence of damming the river?
3. Why do floods still occur, even though people build dams and levees?

Why are these children playing in a fire hydrant?

The deadliest weather phenomena are not blizzards or hurricanes but heat waves. People who are poor or who live in areas where the weather is usually not hot may not have air conditioning. Children have a way of finding a solution to a problem that usually involves fun.

HEAT WAVES

A heat wave is different depending on its location. According to the World Meteorological Organization a region is in a heat wave if it has more than five consecutive days of temperatures that are more than 9oF (5oC) above average. Heat waves have increased in frequency and duration in recent years. The summer 2011 North American heat wave brought record temperatures across the Midwestern and Eastern United States. Many states and localities broke records for temperatures and for most days above 100oF.

CAUSES

A high pressure cell sitting over a region with no movement is the likely cause of a heat wave. What do you think caused the heat wave in the image below (Figure below)? A high pressure zone kept the jet stream further north than normal for August.

A heat wave over the United States as indicated by heat radiated from the ground. The bright yellow areas are the hottest and the blue and white are coolest.

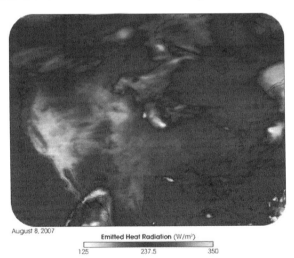

August 8, 2007

Emitted Heat Radiation (W/m²)

125   237.5   350

Droughts

Droughts also depend on what is normal for a region. When a region gets significantly less precipitation than normal for an extended period of time, it is in drought. The Southern United States is experiencing an ongoing and prolonged drought.

Drought has many consequences. When soil loses moisture it may blow away, as happened during the Dust Bowl in the United States in the 1930s. Forests may be lost, dust storms may become common, and wildlife are disturbed. Wildfires become much more common during times of drought.

- It's hard to define a heat wave or a drought because these phenomena depend are deviations from normal conditions in a region.
- A heat wave is caused when a warm high-pressure cell sits over a region.
- Drought may have extremely severe consequences depending on its duration and intensity.

Hurricanes

Hurricanes—called typhoons in the Pacific—are also cyclones. They are cyclones that form in the tropics and so they are also called tropical cyclones. By any name, they are the most damaging storms on Earth.

FORMATION

Hurricanes arise in the tropical latitudes (between 10o and 25oN) in summer and autumn when sea surface temperature are 28oC (82oF) or higher. The warm seas create a large humid air mass. The warm air rises and forms a low pressure cell, known as a tropical depression. Thunderstorms materialize around the tropical depression.

If the temperature reaches or exceeds 28oC (82oF), the air begins to rotate around the low pressure (counterclockwise in the Northern Hemisphere and clockwise in the Southern Hemisphere). As the air rises, water vapor condenses, releasing energy from latent heat. If wind shear is low, the storm builds into a hurricane within two to three days.

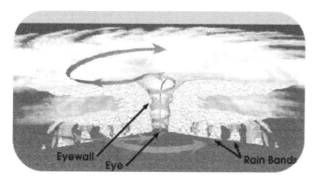

A cross-sectional view of a hurricane.

Hurricanes are huge and produce high winds. The exception is the relatively calm eye of the storm, where air is rising upward. Rainfall can be as high as 2.5 cm (1") per hour, resulting in about 20 billion metric tons of water released daily in a hurricane. The release of latent heat generates enormous amounts of energy, nearly the total annual electrical power consumption of the United States from one storm. Hurricanes can also generate tornadoes.

Hurricanes move with the prevailing winds. In the Northern Hemisphere, they originate in the trade winds and move to the west. When they reach the latitude of the westerlies, they switch direction and travel toward the north or northeast. Hurricanes may cover 800 km (500 miles) in one day.

DAMAGE
Damage from hurricanes comes from the high winds, rainfall, and storm surge. Storm surge occurs as the storm's low pressure center comes onto land, causing the sea level to rise unusually high. A storm surge is often made worse by the hurricane's high winds blowing seawater across the ocean onto the shoreline. Flooding can be devastating, especially along low-lying coastlines such as the Atlantic and Gulf Coasts. Hurricane Camille in 1969 had a 7.3 m (24 foot) storm surge that traveled 125 miles (200 km) inland.

THE END
Hurricanes typically last for 5 to 10 days. The winds push them to the northwest and then to the northeast. Eventually a hurricane will end up over cooler water or land. At that time the hurricane's latent heat source shut downs and the storm weakens. When a hurricane disintegrates, it is replaced with intense rains and tornadoes.
There are about 100 hurricanes around the world each year, plus many smaller tropical storms and tropical depressions. As people develop coastal regions, property damage from storms continues to rise. However, scientists are becoming better at predicting the paths of these storms and fatalities are decreasing. There is, however, one major exception to the previous statement: Hurricane Katrina.

HURRICANE KATRINA

The 2005 Atlantic hurricane season was the longest, costliest, and deadliest hurricane season so far. Total damage from all the storms together was estimated at more than $128 billion, with more than 2,280 deaths. Hurricane Katrina was both the most destructive hurricane and the most costly.

Flooding in New Orleans after Hurricane Katrina caused the levees to break and water to pour through the city.

News about Hurricane Katrina from the New Orleans Times-Picayune:
http://www.nola.com/katrina/graphics/flashflood.swf.

An animation of a radar image of Hurricane Katrina making landfall is seen here:
http://upload.wikimedia.org/wikipedia/commons/9/97/Hurricane_Katrina_LA_landfall_radar.gif.

NASA's short video, "In Katrina's Wake":
http://www.youtube.com/watch?v=HZjqvqaLltl.

Hurricanes are explored in a set of National Geographic videos found at National Geographic Video:
http://video.nationalgeographic.com/video/environment/environment-natural-disasters/hurricanes
At this link, watch the following videos:

- "Hurricanes 101" is an introduction to the topic.
- "How Katrina Formed" looks at the history of Hurricane Katrina as it formed and passed through the Gulf coast.
- Follow that up with "Doomed New Orleans," which explores how the devastation to the city is a man-made disaster.
- "The Hurricane Ike of 1900" looks at what happened in the days when there was little warning before a hurricane hit a coastal city.

Lots of information about hurricanes is found in this online guide from the University of Illinois:
http://ww2010.atmos.uiuc.edu/%28Gh%29/guides/mtr/hurr/home.rxml

SUMMARY

- Hurricanes are actually tropical cyclones because they originate in the tropical latitudes.
- The damage hurricanes cause is due largely to storm surge, but high wind speeds and rain also cause damage.
- Hurricane Katrina was so damaging because the levees that protected New Orleans broke.

WHAT IS A TSUNAMI?

"Tsunami" is a Japanese word meaning "harbor wave." Some people call them tidal waves. But these deadly waves are not related to tides and they are not restricted to harbors. Few words can express the horror these waves can bring.

TSUNAMI AS WAVES

Tsunami are deadly ocean waves from the sharp jolt of an undersea earthquake. Less frequently, these waves can be generated by other shocks to the sea, like a meteorite impact. Fortunately, few undersea earthquakes, and even fewer meteorite impacts, generate tsunami.

WAVE HEIGHT

Tsunami waves have small wave heights relative to their long wavelengths, so they are usually unnoticed at sea. When traveling up a slope onto a shoreline, the wave is pushed upward. As with wind waves, the speed of the bottom of the wave is slowed by friction. This causes the wavelength to decrease and the wave to become unstable. These factors can create an enormous and deadly wave.

How a tsunami forms is shown in this animation:
http://highered.mcgraw-hill.com/olcweb/cgi/pluginpop.cgi?it=swf::640::480::/sites/dl/free/0072402466/30425/16__19.swf::Fig.%2016.19%20-%20Formation%20of%20a%20Tsunami.

Landslides, meteorite impacts, or any other jolt to ocean water may form a tsunami. Tsunami can travel at speeds of 800 kilometers per hour (500 miles per hour).

A video explanation of tsunami is here:
http://www.youtube.com/watch?v=StdqGoezNrY&feature=channel.

WAVELENGTH

Since tsunami are long-wavelength waves, a long time can pass between crests or troughs. Any part of the wave can make landfall first.

In 1755 in Lisbon, Portugal, a tsunami trough hit land first. A large offshore earthquake did a great deal of damage on land. People rushed out to the open space of the shore. Once there, they discovered that the water was flowing seaward fast and some of them went out to observe. What do you think happened next? The people on the open beach drowned when the crest of the wave came up the beach.

Large tsunami in the Indian Ocean and more recently Japan have killed hundreds of thousands of people in recent years. The west coast is vulnerable to tsunami since it sits on the Pacific Ring of Fire. Scientists are trying to learn everything they can about predicting tsunamis before a massive one strikes a little closer to home.
See more at:
http://science.kqed.org/quest/video/scary-tsunamis/.

SUMMARY

- Tsunami have relatively low wave heights, so they are not noticeable until they move up a shore.
- Tsunami have long wavelengths. The time between two crests or two troughs can be many minutes.
- Tsunami warning systems have been placed in most locations where tsunami are possible.

PRACTICE

1. What does the word tsunami mean?
2. Why has Japan had so many tsunamis?
3. What causes a tsunami?
4. How fast do the waves travel?
5. What happens to the tsunami as it reaches the continental shelf?
6. How do tsunamis differ from regular waves?
7. What was the deadliest tsunami ever recorded?
8. What does the Pacific Tsunami Warning Center do?

REVIEW

4. Why is a wave that is so powerful and tall on land unnoticeable at sea?
5. What should you do if you are at the beach and the water suddenly is sucked offshore?
6. Describe tsunami as waves in the way they travel up a shoreline and may strike as crests or troughs.

HUMAN ACTIVITIES THAT CAN CONTRIBUTE TO THE FREQUENCY AND INTENSITY OF NATURAL HAZARDS

How much does your mp3 player really cost? Many of the things we want come partly from minerals. But making minerals useful often causes environmental damage.

MINING AND THE ENVIRONMENT

Although mining provides people with many needed resources, the environmental costs can be high. Surface mining clears the landscape of trees and soil, and nearby streams and lakes are inundated with sediment. Pollutants from the mined rock, such as heavy metals, enter the sediment and water system. Acids flow from some mine sites, changing the composition of nearby waterways (Figure below).

Acid drainage from a surface coal mine in Missouri. U.S. law has changed in recent decades so that a mine region must be restored to its natural state, a process called reclamation. This is not true of older mines. Pits may be refilled or reshaped and vegetation planted. Pits may be allowed to fill with water and become lakes or may be turned into landfills. Underground mines may be sealed off or left open as homes for bats.

- Surface mining clears the land, completely destroying the ecosystems that were found there.
- Mining releases pollutants, which affect the immediate area and may travel downstream or downwind to cause problems elsewhere.
- Reclamation occurs when people attempt to return the mined land to its original state.

What would cause such a tremendous dust storm?

Farmers were forced off their lands during the Dust Bowl in the 1930s when the rains stopped and the topsoil blew off these former grasslands. A wind storm blew huge amounts of soil into the air in Texas on April 14, 1935. This scene was repeated throughout the central United States.

CAUSES OF SOIL EROSION

The agents of soil erosion are the same as the agents of all types of erosion: water, wind, ice, or gravity. Running water is the leading cause of soil erosion, because water is abundant and has a lot of power. Wind is also a leading cause of soil erosion because wind can pick up soil and blow it far away.

Activities that remove vegetation, disturb the ground, or allow the ground to dry are activities that increase erosion. What are some human activities that increase the likelihood that soil will be eroded?

FARMING

Agriculture is probably the most significant activity that accelerates soil erosion because of the amount of land that is farmed and how much farming practices disturb the ground (Figure below). Farmers remove native vegetation and then plow the land to plant new seeds. Because most crops grow only in spring and summer, the land lies fallow during the winter. Of course, winter is also the stormy season in many locations, so wind and rain are available to wash soil away. Tractor tires make deep grooves, which are natural pathways for water. Fine soil is blown away by wind.

The soil that is most likely to erode is the nutrient-rich topsoil, which degrades the farmland.

(a) The bare areas of farmland are especially vulnerable to erosion. (b) Slash-and-burn agriculture leaves land open for soil erosion and is one of the leading causes of soil erosion in the world.

GRAZING

Grazing animals (Figure below) wander over large areas of pasture or natural grasslands eating grasses and shrubs. Grazers expose soil by removing the plant cover for an area. They also churn up the ground with their hooves. If too many animals graze the same land area, the animals' hooves pull plants out by their roots. A land is overgrazed if too many animals are living there.

Grazing animals can cause erosion if they are allowed to overgraze and remove too much or all of the vegetation in a pasture.

LOGGING AND MINING

Logging removes trees that protect the ground from soil erosion. The tree roots hold the soil together and the tree canopy protects the soil from hard falling rain. Logging results in the loss of leaf litter, or dead leaves, bark, and branches on the forest floor. Leaf litter plays an important role in protecting forest soils from erosion (Figure right).

Logging exposes large areas of land to erosion.

Much of the world's original forests have been logged. Many of the tropical forests that remain are currently the site of logging because North America and Europe have already harvested many of their trees (Figure right). Soils eroded from logged forests clog rivers and lakes, fill estuaries, and bury coral reefs.

Deforested swatches in Brazil show up as gray amid the bright red tropical rainforest. Surface mining disturbs the land (Figure below) and leaves the soil vulnerable to erosion.

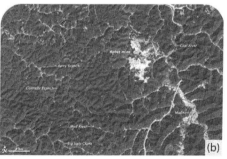

(a) Disturbed land at a coal mine pit in Germany. (b) This coal mine in West Virginia covers more than 10,000 acres (15.6 square miles). Some of the exposed ground is being reclaimed by planting trees.

CONSTRUCTION

Constructing buildings and roads churns up the ground and exposes soil to erosion. In some locations, native landscapes, such as forest and grassland, are cleared, exposing the surface to erosion (in some locations the land that will be built on is farmland). Near construction sites, dirt, picked up by the wind, is often in the air. Completed construction can also contribute to erosion (Figure right).

Urban areas and parking lots result in less water entering the ground. Water runs off the parking lot onto nearby lands and speeds up erosion in those areas.

RECREATIONAL ACTIVITIES

Recreational activities may accelerate soil erosion. Off-road vehicles disturb the landscape and the area eventually develops bare spots where no plants can grow. In some delicate habitats, even hikers' boots can disturb the ground, so it's important to stay on the trail (Figure below).

(a) ATV'S churn up the soil, accelerating erosion. (b) Hiking trails may become eroded.

Soil erosion is as natural as any other type of erosion, but human activities have greatly accelerated soil erosion. In some locations soil erosion may occur about 10 times faster than its natural rate. Since Europeans settled in North America, about one-third of the topsoil in the area that is now the United States has eroded away.

SUMMARY

- Although soil erosion is a natural process, human activities have greatly accelerated it.
- The agents of soil erosion are the same as of other types of erosion: water, ice, wind, and gravity.
- Soil erosion is more likely where the ground has been disturbed by agriculture, grazing animals, logging, mining, construction, and recreational activities.

PRACTICE

Use this resource to answer the questions that follow.

http://www.scalloway.org.uk/phye6.htm

1. What is soil erosion?
2. Where is soil erosion common?
3. How can soil erosion be reduced?
4. What are good farming techniques?
5. What are some natural causes for soil erosion?

REVIEW

6. What is soil erosion? Why did soil erosion accelerate so greatly during the Dust Bowl?
7. How do human activities accelerate soil erosion? Since soil erosion is a natural process, is this bad?
8. What is the consequence of the acceleration of soil erosion?

HUMAN ACTIONS IMPACT THE CARBON CYCLE

Humans have changed the natural balance of the carbon cycle because we use coal, oil, and natural gas to supply our energy demands. Fossil fuels are a sink for CO2 when they form, but they are a source for CO2 when they are burned.

The equation for combustion of propane, which is a simple hydrocarbon looks like this (Figure below):

$$C_3H_8 + 5\,O_2 \rightarrow 3\,CO_2 + 4\,H_2O$$

propane   oxygen   carbon dioxide   water

The equation shows that when propane burns, it uses oxygen and produces carbon dioxide and water. So when a car burns a tank of gas, the amount of CO2 in the atmosphere increases just a little. Added over millions of tanks of gas and coal burned for electricity in power plants and all of the other sources of CO2, the result is the increase in atmospheric CO2 seen in the graph above.

The second largest source of atmospheric CO2 is deforestation (Figure right). Trees naturally absorb CO2 while they are alive. Trees that are cut down lose their ability to absorb CO2. If the tree is burned or decomposes, it becomes a source of CO2. A forest can go from being a carbon sink to being a carbon source.

This forest in Mexico has been cut down and burned to clear forested land for agriculture.

WHY THE CARBON CYCLE IS IMPORTANT

Why is such a small amount of carbon dioxide in the atmosphere even important? Carbon dioxide is a greenhouse gas. Greenhouse gases trap heat energy that would otherwise radiate out into space, which warms Earth. These gases were discussed in Concept

ATMOSPHERIC PROCESSES

This video Keeping up with Carbon from NASA, focuses on the oceans. Topics include what will happen as temperature warms and the oceans can hold less carbon, and ocean acidification: http://www.youtube.com/watch?v=HrIr3xDhQ0E (5:39).

A very thorough but basic summary of the carbon cycle, including the effect of carbon dioxide in the atmosphere, is found in this video:
http://www.youtube.com/watch?v=U3SZKJVKRxQ (4:37).

SUMMARY

- Carbon is essential for life as part of proteins, carbohydrates, and fats.
- The amount of carbon dioxide in the atmosphere is extremely low, but it is extremely important since carbon dioxide is a greenhouse gas, which helps to keep Earth's climate moderate.
- The amount of carbon dioxide in the atmosphere is rising, a fact that has been documented on Mauna Loa volcano since 1958.

WILDFIRES AND HUMANS

The "Utah, Let's Do Our Part" campaign is the result of an interagency effort to reach the public with fire prevention messages relevant to Utah. The program targets three major preventable causes of fires in Utah. They are campfires, debris burning, and vehicle fires. It is the goal of the program to reach specific audiences with fire prevention messages in hopes of reducing the number of human-caused fires in the state. For example, many fires are started by unattended campfires left by teenagers or young adults out for an evening of fun in the mountains. Even on a cold night, campfires can burn all night and turn into major wildfires with a small breeze. The same problem exists with debris burning in the spring and fall. Just because the debris is burned on private land or in a remote corner of a large parcel of land doesn't mean it can be left unattended.

Vehicles are a major problem in Utah because vehicle fires are started in many ways. Often, people pull off the side of the road in the brush to get out of traffic and start fires by the hot cars without the driver ever knowing it. ATVs, trucks, and other vehicles that travel cross country are another major issue as exhaust sparks, dragging metal, hot engines, brake malfunctions, and more cause wildfires.

Source for the above info:
http://www.utahfireinfo.gov/prevention/campaign_info.html

SCIENTISTS USE TECHNOLOGY TO CONTINUALLY IMPROVE ESTIMATES OF WHEN AND WHERE NATURAL HAZARDS OCCUR

What if you could predict an earthquake?

What would make a good prediction? Knowing where, when, and the magnitude of the quake would make it possible for people to evacuate.

A GOOD PREDICTION

Scientists are a long way from being able to predict earthquakes. A good prediction must be detailed and accurate. Where will the earthquake occur? When will it occur? What will be the magnitude of the quake? With a good prediction authorities could get people to evacuate. An unnecessary evacuation is expensive and causes people not to believe authorities the next time an evacuation is ordered.

WHERE?

The probabilities of earthquakes striking along various faults in the San Francisco area between 2003 (when the work was done) and 2032. Where an earthquake will occur is the easiest feature to predict. How would you predict this? Scientists know that earthquakes take place at plate boundaries and tend to happen where they've occurred before (Figure above). Fault segments behave consistently. A segment with frequent small earthquakes or one with infrequent huge earthquakes will likely do the same thing in the future.

WHEN?

When an earthquake will occur is much more difficult to predict. Since stress on a fault builds up at the same rate over time, earthquakes should occur at regular intervals (Figure below). But so far scientists cannot predict when quakes will occur even to within a few years.

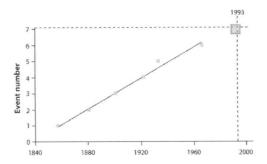

Around Parkfield, California, an earthquake of magnitude 6.0 or higher occurs about every 22 years. So seismologists predicted that one would strike in 1993, but that quake came in 2004 - 11 years late.

EARTHQUAKE SIGNS

Signs sometimes come before a large earthquake. Small quakes, called foreshocks, sometimes occur a few seconds to a few weeks before a major quake. However, many earthquakes do not have foreshocks, and small earthquakes are not necessarily followed by a large earthquake. Ground tilting, caused by the buildup of stress in the rocks, may precede a large earthquake, but not always. Water levels in wells fluctuate as water moves into or out of fractures before an earthquake. This is also an uncertain predictor of large earthquakes. The relative arrival times of P-waves and S-waves also decreases just before an earthquake occurs.

Folklore tells of animals behaving erratically just before an earthquake. Mostly, these anecdotes are told after the earthquake. If indeed animals sense danger from earthquakes or tsunami, scientists do not know what it is they could be sensing, but they would like to find out.

Earthquake prediction is very difficult and not very successful, but scientists are looking for a variety of clues in a variety of locations and to try to advance the field.
See more at http://science.kqed.org/quest/video/earthquakes-breaking-new-ground/.
It's been twenty years since the Loma Prieta Earthquake ravaged downtown Santa Cruz and damaged San Francisco's Marina District and the Bay Bridge. QUEST looks at the dramatic improvements in earthquake prediction technology since 1989. But what can be done with ten seconds of warning?

Find out more by listening to this audio report at:
http://science.kqed.org/quest/audio/predicting-the-next-big-one/.

SUMMARY

- A good prediction must indicate when and where an earthquake will take place with detail and accuracy.
- Fault segments tend to behave the same way over time.
- Signs that an earthquakes may occur include foreshocks, ground tilting, water levels in wells and the relative arrival times of P and S waves.

PRACTICE

1. What magnitude was the 2010 Haiti earthquake?
2. How did scientists recognize that the fault was active?
3. What evidence led to the prediction?
4. What can not be predicted?
5. What type of fault is at the Hayward Fault?

REVIEW

1. Why are earthquakes so hard to predict?
2. Why is it easier to predict where a quake will occur than when?
3. Describe some of the signs that scientists use to predict earthquakes.
4. It's now nine years after the map of earthquake probabilities in the San Francisco Bay area was made. What do you think the fact that no large earthquakes have struck those faults yet does to the probability that one will strike by 2032?

WHAT IS ONE OF THE DEADLIEST SCIENCE JOBS?

No one can predict exactly when a volcanic eruption will take place. There are clues, but no one knows exactly when. Sometimes a volcano will erupt when scientists are studying it. Volcanologists have a high fatality rate among scientists because forecasting eruptions is so difficult.

PREDICTING VOLCANIC ERUPTIONS

Volcanic eruptions can be devastating, particularly to the people who live close to volcanoes. Volcanologists study volcanoes to be able to predict when a volcano will erupt. Many changes happen when a volcano is about to erupt. Even so, eruptions are very difficult to predict.

HISTORY OF VOLCANIC ACTIVITIES

Scientists study a volcano's history to try to predict when it will next erupt. They want to know how long it has been since it last erupted. They also want to know the time span between its previous eruptions. Scientists watch both active and dormant volcanoes closely for signs that show they might erupt.

Mount Rainier in Washington State is currently dormant. The volcano could, and probably will erupt again.

EARTHQUAKES

Earthquakes may take place every day near a volcano. But before an eruption, the number and size of earthquakes increases. This is the result of magma pushing upward into the magma chamber. This motion causes stresses on neighboring rock to build up. Eventually the ground shakes. A continuous string of earthquakes may indicate that a volcano is about to erupt. Scientists use seismographs to record the length and strength of each earthquake.

SLOPE TILT

All that magma and gas pushing upward can make the volcano's slope begin to swell. Ground swelling may change the shape of a volcano or cause rock falls and landslides. Most of the time, the ground tilting is not visible. Scientists detect it by using tiltmeters, which are instruments that measure the angle of the slope of a volcano.

GASES

Scientists measure the gases that escape from a volcano to predict eruptions. Gases like sulfur dioxide (SO_2), carbon dioxide (CO_2), hydrochloric acid (HCl), and water vapor can be measured at the site. Gases may also be measured from satellites. The amounts of gases and the ratios of gases are calculated to help predict eruptions.

REMOTE MONITORING

Satellites can be used to monitor more than just gases (Figure below). Satellites can look for high temperature spots or areas where the volcano surface is changing. This allows scientists to detect changes accurately and safely.

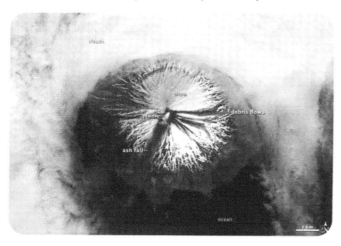

Mount Cleveland, in Alaska, is monitored by satellite.

COSTS AND BENEFITS OF PREDICTIONS

No scientist or government agency wants to announce an eruption and then be wrong. There is a very real cost and disruption to society during a large-scale evacuation. If the scientists are wrong, people would be less likely to evacuate the next time scientists predicted an eruption. But if scientists predict an eruption that does take place, it could save many lives.

SUMMARY

- Volcanologists use several lines of evidence to try to forecast volcanic eruptions.
- Magma moving beneath a volcano will cause earthquakes and slope deformation. Gases may be released from the magma out of the volcano vent.
- Deciding whether to call for an evacuation is very tricky.

PRACTICE

Use the resource below to answer the questions that follow.
Mount Pinatubo: Predicting a Volcanic Eruption at
http://www.teachersdomain.org/asset/ess05_vid_pinatubo/

1. What does the measurement of sulfur dioxide tell scientists?
2. How many seismic stations were established around the mountain?
3. What did the seismic stations measure?
4. What evidence was there for a potential eruption?
5. What finally triggered the evacuation from the island?
6. When did the first eruption occur? How soon after the evacuation?
7. When did the massive eruption occur?

REVIEW

8. What are the signs that magma is moving beneath a volcano?
9. How is a volcano monitored remotely?
10. Why is it helpful for scientists to be able to predict volcanic eruptions?

DOES A PICNIC BRING RAIN?

Weather forecasts are better than they ever have been. According to the World Meteorological Organization (WMO), a 5-day weather forecast today is as reliable as a 2-day forecast was 20 years ago. Now there's no excuse to be rained out on a picnic!

The most accurate weather forecasts are made by advanced computers, with analysis and interpretation added by experienced meteorologists. These computers have up-to-date mathematical models that can use much more data and make many more calculations than would ever be possible by scientists working with just maps and calculators. Meteorologists can use these results to give much more accurate weather forecasts and climate predictions.

In Numerical Weather Prediction (NWP), atmospheric data from many sources are plugged into supercomputers running complex mathematical models (Figure below). The models then calculate what will happen over time at various altitudes for a grid of evenly spaced locations. The grid points are usually between 10 and 200 kilometers apart. Using the results calculated by the model, the program projects weather further into the future. It then uses these results to project the weather still further into the future, as far as the meteorologists want to go. Once a forecast is made, it is broadcast by satellites to more than 1,000 sites around the world.

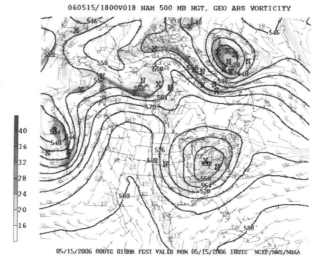

A weather forecast using numerical weather prediction.

NWP produces the most

accurate weather forecasts, but as anyone knows, even the best forecasts are not always right.

Weather prediction is extremely valuable for reducing property damage and even fatalities. If the proposed track of a hurricane can be predicted, people can try to secure their property and then evacuate (Figure below).

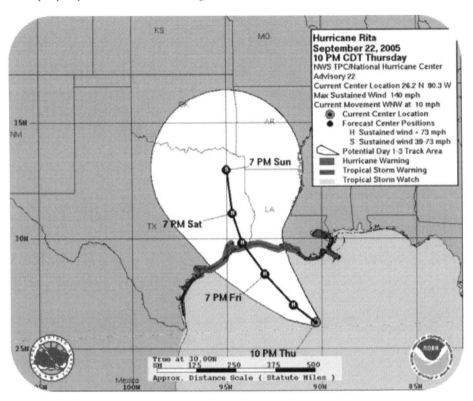

By predicting Hurricane Rita's path, it is likely that lives were saved.

SUMMARY

- Meteorologists use computers to crank data through mathematical models to forecast the weather.
- Numerical weather prediction calculates what will happen to conditions horizontally and vertically over an area.
- Weather forecasts can go further into the future than ever.

PRACTICE

Use this resource to answer the questions that follow.

http://www.youtube.com/watch?v=dqpFU5SRPgY

1. Why is weather difficult to predict?
2. What is the afternoon constellation? What does it do?
3. What are the basic shapes of clouds?
4. What is fog?
5. Why is it important to study clouds?
6. What will Cloudsat do? Why is this an improvement?

REVIEW

7. What is numerical weather prediction?
8. Even with numerical weather prediction, meteorologists have a difficult time predicting the path of a hurricane more than a day or two into the future. Why?
9. One popular online weather prediction site goes 10 days out and another goes 15 days out. Why the discrepancy?

SOCIAL, ECONOMIC, AND ENVIRONMENTAL ISSUES AFFECT DECISIONS ABOUT HUMAN-ENGINEERED STRUCTURES

Use the Internet to investigate and report on a local human engineered structure that is being built (dams, homes, bridges, roads). What kind of social, economic and environmental issues affect the decisions about where these structures are built? Share what you find with a friend.

Made in the USA
Charleston, SC
25 August 2013